Alfred's MUSIC TECH 101

A GROUP STUDY COURSE IN MODERN MUSIC PRODUCTION USING AUDIO TECHNOLOGY

BRIAN LAAKSO

DOWNLOAD FREE CORRELATING MEDIA

Visit **alfred.com/MusicTech101** to download free correlating videos and files for *Alfred's Music Tech 101*. The website also provides periodic updates to keep this book current with the latest info on audio technology. Simply visit **alfred.com/MusicTech101**, and sign in to access files and receive e-mail alerts when new material is added.

Alfred Music
P.O. Box 10003
Van Nuys, CA 91410-0003
alfred.com

Copyright © MMXV by Alfred Music
All rights reserved. Printed in USA.
Produced in association with Lawson Music Media, Inc., Nashville, TN
www.lawsonmusicmedia.com

ISBN-10: 1-4706-1966-0
ISBN-13: 978-1-4706-1966-4

Cover Photo
Digital Music © iStockphoto / teekid

CONTENTS

PART 1

UNIT 1

UNIT 2

Unit 3

Unit 4

Unit 5

Unit 6

Unit 7

Unit 8

PART 3

INDEX

HOW TO USE THIS BOOK

Teachers and students: Please take a moment to read through these instructions so you can effectively kick start a revolution in your music education!

PART 1

The first twelve units (Part 1) of *Music Tech 101* can be used to teach a beginning survey course on music technology. The units are not presented chronologically and can be covered in any order. Each unit contains background reading, student worksheets, a worksheet answer key, and a project or two. There are also video links provided on the companion website for this book: *www.alfred.com/MusicTech101*.

Unit Reading: These sections are geared toward both teachers and students. They provide background knowledge on the unit. The teacher must read these, but if there is limited class time it is not necessary (and may not be practical) for the student to read them.

Student Worksheet: These focus on the fundamental concepts. that will help students understand the topics covered in the unit. The questions are designed to stand independently of the Unit Reading and are not intended to assess the understanding of the reading. In fact, it's even possible to cover the worksheet without requiring students to engage with the reading. Again, this is useful if there is limited class time.

Answers/Study Guide: These are essentially a key, containing the answers to the questions on the Student Worksheet.

Unit Project: These are hands-on interactive projects that should take up the majority of class contact time. They are lengthy and involved, and are designed to span multiple class periods on multiple days. It is essential for completed projects to be shared with the class. Students love to hear what other students have done and will be very supportive of each other when it comes to music making.

Supplemental Materials: Available on the book's companion website (*www.alfred. com/MusicTech101*) are PowerPoint files that accompany the Student Worksheets, as well other materials (like video links) that really help the book come alive. These are an integral part of the book, and it is strongly recommended that you share these videos with students.

What a Typical Course Week Might Look Like

Sunday .... The teacher reads the Unit Reading to get some background knowledge. The teacher selects videos from the book's companion website to share.

Monday .... The teacher uses PowerPoint to cover the questions on the Student Worksheet. The teacher shows videos from the companion website to make the unit come alive. The students take notes on the material using the Student Worksheet.

Tuesday .... Students and teacher review the material. Perhaps a supplemental video is shown. Students begin work on the Unit Project.

Wednesday .... Students and teacher review the material. Perhaps a supplemental video is shown. Students continue work on the Unit Project.

Thursday .... Students and teacher review the material. Perhaps a supplemental video is shown. Students finish work on the Unit Project.

Friday .... Students take the Unit Test (a blank Student Worksheet doubles as the Test). Students share finished projects with each other.

PART 2

The next section of this book (Part 2) can be used to teach a beginning songwriting/multimedia course on music technology. The projects in this section are more advanced and targeted for more experienced students. They are not chronological and can be covered in any order.

Project Work: This section consists of hands-on interactive projects that should take up the majority of class contact time. They are more lengthy and involved than any projects in Part 1, and are designed to span a week or more per project.

Daily Effort Assessment: It can be difficult to engage with a long-term project. To help keep everyone on track, students should self-assess their effort level at the end of each class. This becomes part of their grade. It is effective for them to self-evaluate daily based on the following point scale.

Effort/Creativity/Focus Grading Rubric

0–5 points .... I did almost nothing and put forth extremely low effort.

6–10 points .... I did a little more than the minimum and put forth just a little effort.

11–15 points. ..... I worked with average creativity and put forth average effort.

16–20 points. ..... I did great work, had great focus, and put forth great effort.

21–25 points. ..... I did top-notch work, showed superior creativity, and put forth excellent effort.

Sharing: It is essential that once projects are completed that they be shared with the class. Students love to hear what other students have done, and they are very supportive of each other when it comes to music making. When sharing projects at this level, kids should be developing critical listening skills. There should be engaging conversations about the music.

Guiding questions for conversation might include:

1. What specifically was successful about this piece?
2. What would take this piece to the next level?
3. What could be added, subtracted, or changed to improve the piece?
4. Were all the requirements for the project met?
5. What was learned from completing the project?

PART 3

The final section of this book gives students great freedom of choice in their own educational experience. There is only one set of guidelines for projects in this section, but there are many paths to learning. Part 3 is designed for experienced students who are capable of a high level of independent study. Students must be able to play both roles of teacher and student. They must create their own learning goals, plan how to achieve them, and follow through with the assignment they have given themselves.

Project Work: These hands-on interactive projects should take up the majority of class contact time. They are more lengthy and involved than any projects in Part 1 or Part 2, and are designed to span two weeks or more per project.

Daily Effort Assessment: Please follow the instructions outlined in Part 2. Students will self-evaluate daily based on the 0–25 point scale from Part 2.

Sharing: Please follow the instructions outlined in Part 2. Students will share their projects with each other and engage in meaningful conversation about their work.

Website / Audio Information

Music Tech 101 is intended to be a curriculum that is ready for almost any music class. An expensive studio and fancy gear are not required, and most software referenced here is free or very inexpensive.

When using a website with a large class or multiple classes, create a single profile and login for your school (e.g., username: "RooseveltHigh" / password: "MusicTech"). Students can title their projects by name, like "Brian's Song." This way, all projects will be stored in one account, making it very easy to grade or share songs from the comfort of one computer.

Some projects in this book require a student to record music from a website. The tools used to accomplish this is slightly different between Windows and Mac users.

Windows users: Two programs that can capture audio from a website are *Audacity* (free) and *Mixcraft* (inexpensive). Enter the Preferences menu for each program to change the "Recording Input / Devices" source to Stereo Mix (this has to be enabled in your system). Hit the "Record" button in your software, jump over to the website and play the audio, then go back to your software and hit the "Stop" button. Voila! A recording.

Mac users: Download a program like *SoundFlower*, which will route audio from a website to a recording program like

GarageBand or Audacity (both free). Within SoundFlower's Audio Devices, ensure that SoundFlower is the default and system output. Then set the "Recording Input/Devices" source within GarageBand or Audacity to record from SoundFlower. You can then hit the "Record" button in your software, jump over to the website and play the audio, then come back to your software and hit the "Stop" button. Voila! A recording.

Note from the Author
We encourage you to use the material here to develop your own lesson plans and projects. Check out supplemental YouTube videos on your own—there is always new content being created! Find your own music making websites to explore with students. Fresh sites appear (and sometimes disappear) every week.

Allow your students to share information about these topics—this will help make the learning experience richer, more relevant, and engaging. Give them credit for their contributions, and share them!

If you need technical assistance, pedagogical advice, have questions, or just want to strike up a conversation about music and technology, feel free to email me at *blaakso@ gmail.com.*

Thanks and have fun while you learn. Now, let's begin with kick starting a revolution in your music education!

–Brian Laakso

Figure I.1

PART 1

FUNDAMENTALS

Part 1 of *Music Tech 101* covers the fundamentals of music technology and gives you the opportunity to create, share, discuss, read, write about, and listen to music made with technology. You'll actively use technology to explore these elements as you investigate a broad range of topics. We will focus primarily on the history and possible futures of technology and its impact on the world of music. Part 1 covers topics like audio editing, sequencing software, remixing, sound systems, the modern music business, studio recording, synthesizers, copyright law, DJing, recording media, electric guitars, video-game music, and other contemporary themes.

Goals for Part 1

- Write your own rap
- Create beats on the computer
- Make a radio commercial
- Remix songs
- Learn about the modern music business
- Create your own DJ mixtape
- Analyze how your favorite song was made
- Write music online
- Create your own record label

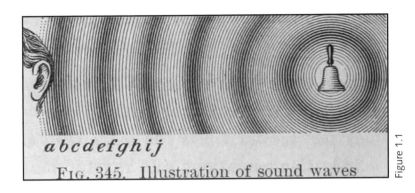

Figure 1.1

UNIT 1
THE SCIENCE OF SOUND

UNIT READING

Studying the physics of sound is a fundamental place to get started understanding concepts. in music technology. Knowing how sound waves work provides the basis for thinking about early synthesizers, electricity, and the beginning of electronic music.

SOUND WAVES

First, let's start by understanding the *electromagnetic spectrum.* There are two types of electromagnetic waves: *mechanical* (which must travel through a medium) and *electromagnetic* (which can travel through a vacuum). The lowest and largest electromagnetic waves, with the smallest amount of energy, are sound waves—while radio and television waves are a bit more intense. Microwaves, mobile phones, radars, and remote controls occupy the next few tiers of energy, followed by visible light. X-rays and gamma rays occupy the most energetic segment of the spectrum.

Frequency

The *frequency* of a sound wave describes the number of times it vibrates per second. A popular reference frequency is A = 440 hertz, which is the A above middle C on the piano keyboard. For this particular A, the piano string vibrates at 440 *hertz* (cycles per second, abbreviated as *Hz*). Piano tuners use this tone as a reference for tuning a piano—doubling the number to 880Hz produces the A note one octave (eight notes) higher, and 220Hz is one octave lower. Frequencies are important to understand because they ultimately indicate how high or how low a particular note is—an important concept for synthesizers, since they produce notes with electricity. (We will be discussing synthesizers later in this unit.) Humans can hear sounds within the range of 20Hz to 20,000Hz (or, 20kHz). Once sounds are released into the atmosphere, the particles push against each other, travel through the air, and reach our eardrums, which vibrate at the same rate. Our ears then convert these vibrations into electrical signals, which our brains perceive as sound. The speed of sound changes depending upon what material it travels through. When a supersonic jet reaches Mach 1, it will be going faster than the speed of sound through air, which is 768 miles per hour.

Ultrasound

Extremely high frequencies above our hearing range are called *ultrasound* and have many practical applications apart from music. Animals, such as bats and dolphins, use ultrasound for echolocation to detect their prey. Medical sonography uses ultrasound to help visualize parts of the body, including muscles, organs, and babies in the womb. And ultrasonic cleaners can get rid of tiny particles of dirt on jewelry or medical equipment.

Infrasound

Extremely low frequencies below our hearing range are called *infrasound* and have frequent occurrences in both the natural and industrial world. Earthquakes, volcanic activity, and heavy surf all produce infrasound and can be sensed a few miles away by animals and instruments, such as a seismograph, to warn of possible danger. Some animals, such as elephants and alligators, use infrasound to communicate with each other over the distance of several miles. And some factory equipment and heating systems produce infrasound at high decibels when in operation. These sounds are very low, often undetectable by the human ear, but they have been known to cause illness and headaches with workers.

Decibel

The *decibel* (dB) level of a sound wave describes the intensity of the sound's frequency at a given distance—or, more simply put, a sound's volume. Normal speech falls around 60dB to 70dB, a lawn mower outputs around 100dB, sounds start to feel painful at about 125dB, and hearing loss can occur at around 180dB. It is even possible to break a drinking glass using only the human voice—if the sound is concentrated onto a very narrow area, the decibel level is high enough, and the singer matches the exact resonant frequency of the glass. There was an episode of the TV show *MythBusters* dedicated to this experiment.

Waveforms

Sound waves can travel in different forms. Their cycles may vary in shape, and in turn the resultant sounds of different waves can be radically dissimilar. *Sawtooth-shaped waves* produce the bright, brassy timbre of a trumpet. *Sine waves,* with their gentle and even slopes, produce a sound similar to a flute. *Square waves* sound like wind instruments, such as a clarinet. Early electronic keyboard instruments, like the Minimoog, used these different waveforms to imitate the sounds of acoustic instruments, though their tones nevertheless remained distinctly electronic. These early electronic keyboards created, modified, and combined various waveforms to generate new sounds never before heard! This is why many keyboards were referred to as *synthesizers*.

Acoustics

The study of the way sound travels is called *acoustics*. It's important to understand this science, especially when designing recording studios and concert halls. In a recording studio, walls may intersect at odd angles (to prevent the reflection of sound), or they may be extra thick and covered with soundproofing material (to prevent sounds from entering or escaping the environment). This causes a room to be acoustically "dead" and is advantageous in a studio because it enables the recording engineer to capture a very clean, isolated portrait of instruments or singers. In a concert hall, sound needs to travel some distance to reach all members of the audience, yet the hall cannot be constructed in a way that allows echoing sound to interfere with the clarity of what is heard. As a result, acoustic technicians, or acousticians, must understand mathematically and architecturally how to construct various spaces to suit the room's purpose.

Radio Waves

A final topic for this unit is radio, and specifically, *radio waves.* Radio originated as a wireless form of communication around the beginning of the 1900s. There are four basic kinds of radio transmission: *AM* (amplitude modulation), *FM* (frequency modulation), *HD* (high definition), and *satellite.* Each of these carries music on radio waves that constantly bombard our bodies from every direction. However, to detect the waves, you must use the right kind of antenna and receiver. It's pretty amazing to think that radio enables invisible music to travel through the air!

Most radio waves are used for one-way communication. However, *ham radio* (amateur radio) is intended for private use and can support long-distance communication among multiple parties, while *CB* (citizens band) radio is used for localized communication between individuals.

Figure 1.2 Vocalists Joan Weldon and Byron Palmer

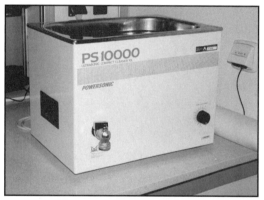

Figure 1.3 Laboratory ultrasonic bath

Figure 1.4 *Tsunami* by Hokusai, 1826

STUDENT WORKSHEET

1. What term describes the number of vibrations per second of a frequency?

2. What is the range of frequencies the human ear can detect?

3. A man's voice has a certain frequency range. A woman's voice occupies another frequency range. Which voice vibrates at a faster rate?

   (See Figure 1.2)

4. Name the term for extremely high frequencies.

5. What animal can detect the highest frequency sounds?

6. What practical purpose do ultrasonic waves serve? *(See Figure 1.3)*

7. Name the term for extremely low frequencies.

8. What animal can detect the lowest frequency sounds?

Figure 1.5 Tuning fork

9. What practical purpose do infrasonic waves serve? *(See Figure 1.4)*

10. Music is based on blending different frequencies. If a tuning fork vibrates at 1000Hz, at what rate would another fork need to vibrate to sound an octave (eight notes) lower? *(See Figure 1.5)*

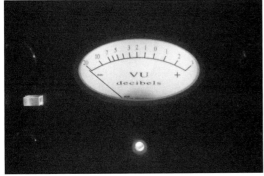

Figure 1.6 VU decibel meter

11. Describe in simple terms how your ears function.

12. What do decibels (dB) measure? *(See Figure 1.6)*

Figure 1.7 A U.S. Navy jet breaks the sound barrier

13. At what approximate decibel level do the following occur?

    a. Quiet conversation

    b. A power mower

    c. Pain

    d. Actual hearing loss

Figure 1.8 Resonant frequencies can break glass

14. The speed of sound changes depending upon the material it travels through. When a supersonic jet reaches Mach 1, it will be going faster than the speed of sound through air. How fast is that? *(See Figure 1.7)*

Figure 1.9 Acoustics of a large concert hall

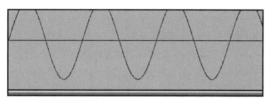

Figure 1.10 50Hz sine wave

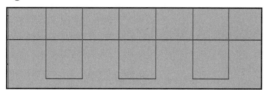

Figure 1.11 50Hz square wave

Figure 1.12 50Hz sawtooth wave

Figure 1.13 An antique radio

15. How can a singer break a drinking glass with his or her voice? *(See Figure 1.8)*

16. What are acoustics and why are they important in studios and concert halls? *(See Figure 1.9)*

17. Early synthesizers produced different kinds of sound waves in an effort to imitate actual musical instruments. Name *two* types of waves and the musical instruments they sound closest to. *(See Figures 1.10–1.12)*

18. What does it mean to synthesize something?

19. Radio was invented in the early 1900s. Name *three* kinds of radio transmission. *(See Figure 1.13)*

20. What is ham radio?

Figure 1.2 Vocalists Joan Weldon and Byron Palmer

Figure 1.3 Laboratory ultrasonic bath

Figure 1.4 *Tsunami* by Hokusai, 1826

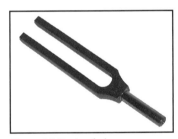

Figure 1.5 Tuning fork

Figure 1.6 VU decibel meter

ANSWERS/STUDY GUIDE

1. What term describes the number of vibrations per second of a frequency?

   Hertz (Hz)

2. What is the average range of frequencies the human ear can detect?

   20Hz to 20kHz

3. A man's voice has a certain frequency range. A woman's voice occupies another frequency range. Which voice vibrates at a faster rate?

   A woman's voice because it is higher

4. Name the term for extremely high frequencies.

   Ultrasound

5. What animal can detect the highest frequency sounds?

   Bats or dolphins

6. What practical purpose do ultrasonic waves serve? *(See Figure 1.3)*

   Cleaning jewelry, detecting babies in the womb

7. Name the term for extremely low frequencies.

   Infrasound

8. What animal can detect the lowest frequency sounds?

   Elephants or alligators

9. What practical purpose do infrasonic waves serve? *(See Figure 1.4)*

   Detecting earthquakes. Whales and elephants also use them to communicate.

10. Music is based on blending different frequencies. If a tuning fork vibrates at 1000Hz, at what rate would another fork need to vibrate to sound an octave (eight notes) lower? *(See Figure 1.5)*

    500Hz

11. Describe in simple terms how your ears function.

    They collect vibrations and convert them into electrical signals that your brain interprets as sound

12. What do decibels (dB) measure? *(See Figure 1.6)*

Figure 1.7 A U.S. Navy jet breaks the sound barrier

Figure 1.8 Resonant frequencies can break glass

Figure 1.9 Acoustics of a large concert hall

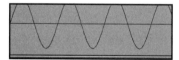

Figure 1.10 50Hz sine wave

Figure 1.11 50Hz square wave

Figure 1.12 50Hz sawtooth wave

Figure 1.13 An antique radio

Sound intensity or volume level

13. At what approximate decibel level do the following occur?

    a. Quiet conversation: *60dB to 70dB*

    b. Power mower: *100dB*

    c. Pain: *125dB*

    d. Actual hearing loss: *180dB*

14. The speed of sound changes depending upon what material it travels through. When a supersonic jet reaches Mach 1, it will be going faster than the speed of sound through air. How fast is that? *(See Figure 1.7)*

    More than 700 MPH (768 MPH, to be specific) or 343 meters per second

15. How can a singer break a glass with his or her voice? *(See Figure 1.8)*

    He or she must match the resonant frequency (Hz) of the glass, sing with enough power (dB), and allow the vibrations to build up until the glass cracks.

16. What are acoustics and why are they important in studios and concert halls? *(See Figure 1.9)*

    Acoustics are the study of the way sound travels. It's important to design these rooms to control the direction of sound, prevent echoing, and keep out exterior sounds.

17. Early synthesizers produced different kinds of sound waves in an effort to imitate actual musical instruments. Name *two* types of waves and the musical instruments they sound closest to. *(See Figures 1.10–1.12)*

    Sine: flute
    Square: clarinet
    Sawtooth: trumpet

18. What does it mean to synthesize something?

    To create, modify, and combine various waveforms to generate new sounds

19. Radio was invented in the early 1900s. Name *three* kinds of radio transmission. *(See Figure 1.12)*

    AM, FM, ham, high definition, satellite, citizens band (CB)

20. What is ham radio?

    Amateur radio for private use

UNIT PROJECT

YOUR MISSION

Write a song or rap by yourself or with a partner that describes something you learned from Unit 1. Use the WD-1 website (www.worteldrie.com/WD-1) to provide the music. You can write music first and then lyrics, or lyrics and then music.

Resource

www.worteldrie.com/WD-1   ✗

Music

Follow these steps to help with writing music for your Unit Project:

1. Go to the WD-1 website: www.worteldrie.com/WD-1.

2. Choose a style of music you like and a beat that you can write lyrics to.

3. Use the keyboard and mouse to "play" the WD-1 live, and try to develop a song.

4. The song must use the following format. Use the keys to play some funky stuff!

   - Intro
   - Verse 1
   - Chorus
   - Verse 2
   - Chorus
   - Outro

5. Practice the song. If you need to, take notes on which keys you are pressing.

6. Open Mixcraft, GarageBand, Audacity, or another recording software, and record your song.

Lyrics

Use the following guide to help with writing lyrics for your Unit Project:

   - Verse 1: 4 lines
   - Chorus: 4 lines
   - Verse 2: 4 lines
   - Chorus: Repeated
   - The lyrics should rhyme and can be spoken, rapped, or sung.
   - The lyrics should include five topics or facts from the notes of this unit.
   - You can sneak facts in any way you'd like—be creative!
   - Work quickly, efficiently, and smartly, since you'll have limited time to work on this song.
   - Create a solid beginning and ending for extra polish. The total time of the song should be less than three minutes.

Grading

25 points ....Use the WD-1 interatively, with changes/builds/breakdowns and so on.

25 points ....Include five topics/facts in the lyrics (5 points each).

25 points ....Proper structure:

> Intro ....2.5 points
> Verse 1 ....5 points
> Chorus ....5 points
> Verse 2 ....5 points
> Chorus ....5 points
> Outro ....2.5 points

25 points ....Record the music and lyrics in Mixcraft, GarageBand, or Audacity and save them as an MP3 to share.

─────────────────────────────

100 points ....*Totally awesome!*

Extra Credit

+20 points ....Perform it live with your partner in class.

+20 points ....Use some kind of effects on the song after it has been recorded.

+5 points ....Write an additional verse (5 points for each additional verse you write).

Figure 2.2 First instrument with mechanical gears

Figure 2.3 Device that transmits Morse code

Figure 2.4 Piano from 1885

Figure 2.5 A professional thereminist

STUDENT WORKSHEET

1. What type of early automatic instrument could play music without a human's touch?

2. What was the first instrument to use gear technology? (It was cranked.) *(See Figure 2.2)*

3. What invention from 1832 could play a single audible tone using electrical current—and used those tones to communicate with Morse code? (It would later inspire electronic keyboards.) *(See Figure 2.3)*

4. What machine, invented in the late 1800s, allowed users to listen to any song at any time by loading rolls of paper into it? *(See Figure 2.4)*

5. What instrument created in the late 1900s could play *any* kind of music?

6a. Why is the theremin (from 1920) so unusual?

6b. What do each of the two metal bars on the theremin control? *(See Figure 2.5)*

Figure 2.6 Classic Minimoog

Figure 2.7 Fairlight CMI

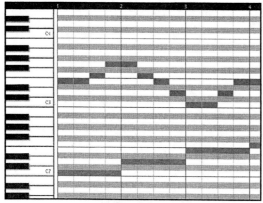
Figure 2.8 Piano roll of Beethoven's *Ode to Joy*

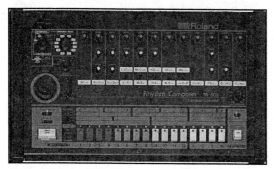
Figure 2.9 Roland TR-808

7. In 1964, Bob Moog invented the first electricity-driven keyboard. It was like hooking up telegraphs in a row: low voltage = low notes and high voltage = high notes. *(See Figure 2.6)*

   a. In 1971, a portable version of this keyboard was made. What was it called?

   b. How is it still relevant?

   c. Name two artists who use it to make music.

8. Name two things that were special about 1979's Fairlight CMI. *(See Figure 2.7)*

9. Name two artists that paid $20,000 for the Fairlight CMI.

10. Musical Instrument Digital Interface (MIDI) was invented in 1980. What did it do? *(See Figure 2.8)*

11. Where is MIDI used besides music?

12. What is a sequencer?

13a. What type of Roland drum sequencer was used in old-school hip-hop/dance music?

13b. Who uses it to make music—and even named an album after it? *(See Figure 2.9)*

Figure 2.10 Pro Tools in a professional studio

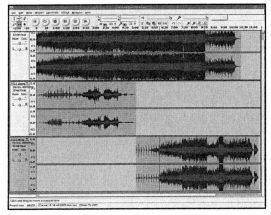

Figure 2.11 Audacity screenshot

Figure 2.12 Native Instruments Maschine

Figure 2.13 DJ controller system

14a. What kind of sequencer is Avid's Pro Tools?

14b. What is it used for?

15. What could Pro Tools be compared to in the writing world? The art world? *(See Figure 2.10)*

16. How does a digital sequencer like Pro Tools give musicians total control over a song?

17. Name one other popular sequencer.

18. Name a free sequencer you can get online.

19. Reason and FL Studio are also popular sequencers. How does each of them work?

20. Maschine, the MPC, and the Korg padKONTROL are examples of what? *(See Figure 2.12)*

21. Name the software package, originally released in 2000, that revolutionized DJing and allowed DJs to mix, scratch, sample, and beat-match MP3s. *(See Figure 2.13)*

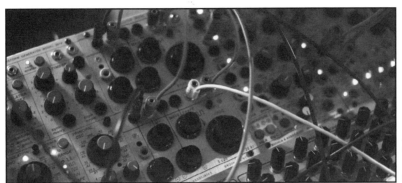

Figure 2.1

UNIT 2
AMAZING INSTRUMENTS OF MUSIC TECHNOLOGY

UNIT READING

There are many amazing instruments of music technology. In this unit, we'll explore a small sampling of some of the most interesting and unusual musical instruments that have developed as a result of technology. Some are now footnotes in music history, and some have been modified and continue to be useful today.

EARLY MUSIC TECHNOLOGY

The first instrument that could play itself without any kind of human intervention was the *windchimes,* which has roots in Italy, Japan, India, and China as early as 1100 BC. Although this may not seem like technology by today's standards, the fact that windchimes could create music unaided by humans was pretty incredible.

Gears

Another step in technology was the use of gears. The *hurdy gurdy* might be considered the first instrument that used gears to create music. It was operated by a crank that rotated against a set of strings. The earliest hurdy gurdy was called an *organistrum* and originated in the tenth century.

The Telegraph

Although not originally created to be a musical instrument, the *telegraph* (1832) produced a specific pitch that might be considered musical. Telegraphs are simple electrical circuits that communicate by sending electricity down a wire that can be hundreds of miles long! *Morse code,* developed by American inventor Samuel Morse, assigned a series of long and short sounds to each letter of the alphabet as a means to communicate across the distance.

These varying lengths of tone gave the pitch some rhythm, and in a sense the telegraph could therefore be considered a predecessor of an individual keyboard key.

Player Piano

The late 1800s brought *player pianos* to the public. Originally operated by foot pumps (and later electricity), these pianos cranked through rolls of paper that had been pierced with holes. The holes triggered notes on the piano to play automatically. An owner of a player piano could go to the store to purchase songs by the roll, bring them home, and entertain guests with them. American composer Conlon Nancarrow tried to push the machine (and the piano) to its limits. He would create his own piano rolls, except he tried poking as many holes into them as possible. This drove the piano machine to play complex rhythms and polytonalities that would be impossible for a human to actually play. Recordings of this music are pretty bizarre and haunting. Other recent composers have applied the same technique to MIDI keyboards, creating songs that demand the machine to play millions of notes within a few minutes, in a new genre known as *black MIDI*. We'll talk more about MIDI shortly.

Radio

The *radio* may not be considered a musical instrument, but it certainly is an amazing machine of music technology. Just think about it: a radio is a box that picks up invisible music from the air and puts that music back together in audio form for listeners. Radio was first created in the early 1900s, when listeners tuned in to various stations based on their musical interests and often gathered in groups to listen together. It's pretty amazing that radio is still popular more than 100 years after its invention.

Theremin

In 1920, Russian scientist Léon Theremin created an instrument that became known as the *theremin*. Theremins had two perpendicular bars protruding from a small box. The bars created an energy field that, when interrupted by a human hand, would create a tone. Moving a hand vertically next to the bar raised and lowered the pitch; moving a hand horizontally toward and away from the bar controlled the volume. Theremins were popular for their unusual sound and known especially for the fact that they did not need to be touched to be played. They found their way into popular culture via the Beach Boys (used in "Good Vibrations"), *Scooby-Doo* (used as the sound of creepy ghosts), Led Zeppelin, and Marilyn Manson. Build-your-own-theremin kits are still available for around $300.

Bob Moog

American scientist Bob Moog made his early living from the sale of theremins. His interest in electronics inspired him to create his own electronic keyboard. His principle was fairly simple. With a telegraph, different pitches could be created based on changing the amounts of electrical current passing through the wire. High currents yielded high pitches, and low currents yielded low pitches. Moog figured that if he basically set up a few dozen telegraphs in a row, each delivering a slightly different current, he could create an electronic keyboard—the *Moog keyboard*.

Moog built his first keyboards as purely *analog*—all the sounds were created by modifying electrical current. Moog keyboards had the ability to produce different kinds of sound waves—square, sine, triangle, and sawtooth. The user could control overtones as well as different kinds of filters. The sounds the Moog produced were unlike anything ever heard before. It became known as a *synthesizer* because it put together sounds that had never before been combined in the history of music!

Minimoog

In 1969, Bob Moog developed a small, portable version of the Moog called the *Minimoog*. The Minimoog has enjoyed quite a bit of popularity and is still used in many of today's hip-hop and dance hits. People may not recognize the Minimoog, but they likely recognize its sound. Artists such as Jay-Z, Lil Jon, Snoop Dogg, the Black Eyed Peas, and Madonna have all used the Minimoog on albums or onstage.

DIGITAL SAMPLING SYNTHESIZERS

The *Fairlight CMI* was the very first digital sampling synthesizer. It didn't just produce sounds using electricity, it also could actually record sounds (using a microphone) and play them back at different pitches using the keyboard. It was the first musical instrument with a computer screen and a hard drive attached to it, and it had a special light pen and drawing tablet for users to interact with the features. CMIs were extremely expensive, costing about $20,000 back in 1979. Stevie Wonder, Prince, Michael Jackson, and Queen were a few artists who could afford to use the CMI in their music.

MIDI

As more and more electronic instruments began to gain popularity, musicians really wanted to be able to link them together to create more complex instrumentation. The solution for syncing up machines came via *MIDI,* or *Musical Instrument Digital Interface*. This allowed multiple synthesizers to be linked together via a MIDI cable (much like today's USB connectors) so that they could be played simultaneously.

MIDI also allowed any properly equipped keyboard to trigger and play sounds in other keyboards. MIDI's capabilities extended to rack-mounted synthesizers and samplers (musical box units without keys), and even sounds stored in a computer.

Today, MIDI is used in many applications other than music. It controls scenic theatre lighting sequences for plays and musicals, and it triggers the animatronic robots at Disney theme parks. MIDI also provides communication about player interactions between game consoles and musical controllers in the worlds of *Rock Band, Guitar Hero*, and *DJ Hero*.

SEQUENCERS

Next, let's discuss *sequencers*. A sequencer is basically a piece of hardware or software that creates, manages, and plays music in a particular order. Simple kinds of sequencers include drum machines and multitrack recording programs.

Hardware Sequencers

We'll first discuss *hardware sequencers*. Hardware is a physical The *Roland TR-808* drum machine is probably the most popular drum machine sequencer ever created. Originally hitting the market in 1980, this little metallic box was a key influence in many styles of music, including R&B, dance, and hip-hop. In fact, it was the first drum machine featured in a hip-hop song—Afrika Bambaataa's "Planet Rock." It also inspired more recent hip-hop albums, such as Kanye West's *808s & Heartbreak*, which featured an 808 on every track. Other artists that have used an 808 in their music include Jay-Z, Outkast, Lil Wayne, the Black Eyed Peas, Public Enemy, and Britney Spears. Other popular Roland hardware sequencers include models TR-909 (drum machine) and TB-303 (bass sequencer).

Software Sequencers

Avid's Pro Tools is currently the most popular *software sequencer*. (Software can be defined as instructions that direct a computer to perform specific instructions—as opposed to hardware, which is a physical object that interacts with a computer to perform tasks.) Pro Tools is used in most of today's recording studios. It has been used in countless studios to record many different styles of music. Also known as a *digital audio workstation* (or *DAW*), it gives recording engineers and producers complete control over every aspect of the music. It can be used to fix wrong notes, add effects, blend hundreds of tracks, and more. Think about this parallel: Microsoft Word allows users to change font styles, sizes, and colors; cut and paste portions of text; insert pictures; and use many other features. Pro Tools does this for music. Adobe Photoshop allows users to modify pictures by correcting colors, smoothing out blemishes, enhancing lighting, and helping photos look perfect. Pro Tools does this for music—it can help music to sound "perfect."

Other popular software sequencers include GarageBand, ACID, Audacity, Mixcraft, Logic, Ableton Live, REAPER, and Audition. FL Studio allows musicians to create, edit, and arrange loops of music, much like building a structure with Lego bricks. Reason is a virtual studio where musicians can build cool sounds, effects, and songs from scratch.

Hybrid Sequencers

A few sequencers hitting the market are a hybrid of hardware and software sequencers. One example is *Maschine* by Native Instruments, a hardware controller that interacts with software via pads, buttons, and knobs. You can load combinations of sounds to be triggered by tapping each of the 16 pressure-sensitive drum pads. When you hook it up to a DAW, such as Ableton Live, you can instantly create entire songs onstage. Maschine, the MPC, and the Korg padKONTROL are all examples of MIDI *pad controllers*.

Another hardware/software package by Native Instruments, originally released in 2000, revolutionized DJing. *Traktor Scratch Pro* allows DJs to mix, scratch, sample, and beat-match MP3s. DJs can also grab loops from any point in a song and jam with them, combine them, and create new songs out of smaller fragments.

There are many amazing instruments of music technology; these are just a few highlights across the timeline of musical evolution.

Figure 2.2 First instrument with mechanical gears

Figure 2.3 Device that transmits Morse code

Figure 2.4 Piano from 1885

Figure 2.5 A professional thereminist

STUDENT WORKSHEET

1. What type of early automatic instrument could play music without a human's touch?

2. What was the first instrument to use gear technology? (It was cranked.) *(See Figure 2.2)*

3. What invention from 1832 could play a single audible tone using electrical current—and used those tones to communicate with Morse code? (It would later inspire electronic keyboards.) *(See Figure 2.3)*

4. What machine, invented in the late 1800s, allowed users to listen to any song at any time by loading rolls of paper into it? *(See Figure 2.4)*

5. What instrument created in the late 1900s could play *any* kind of music?

6a. Why is the theremin (from 1920) so unusual?

6b. What do each of the two metal bars on the theremin control? *(See Figure 2.5)*

Figure 2.6 Classic Minimoog

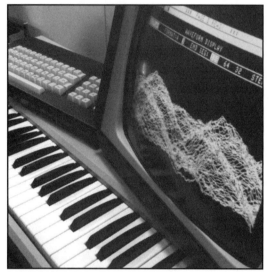

Figure 2.7 Fairlight CMI

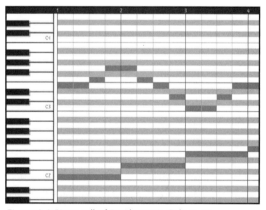

Figure 2.8 Piano roll of Beethoven's *Ode to Joy*

Figure 2.9 Roland TR-808

7. In 1964, Bob Moog invented the first electricity-driven keyboard. It was like hooking up telegraphs in a row: low voltage = low notes and high voltage = high notes. *(See Figure 2.6)*

   a. In 1971, a portable version of this keyboard was made. What was it called?

   b. How is it still relevant?

   c. Name two artists who use it to make music.

8. Name two things that were special about 1979's Fairlight CMI. *(See Figure 2.7)*

9. Name two artists that paid $20,000 for the Fairlight CMI.

10. Musical Instrument Digital Interface (MIDI) was invented in 1980. What did it do? *(See Figure 2.8)*

11. Where is MIDI used besides music?

12. What is a sequencer?

13a. What type of Roland drum sequencer was used in old-school hip-hop/dance music?

13b. Who uses it to make music—and even named an album after it? *(See Figure 2.9)*

Figure 2.10 Pro Tools in a professional studio

14a. What kind of sequencer is Avid's Pro Tools?

14b. What is it used for?

15. What could Pro Tools be compared to in the writing world? The art world? *(See Figure 2.10)*

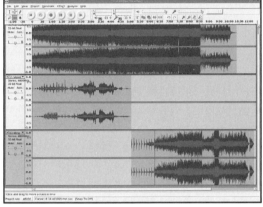

Figure 2.11 Audacity screenshot

16. How does a digital sequencer like Pro Tools give musicians total control over a song?

17. Name one other popular sequencer.

18. Name a free sequencer you can get online.

Figure 2.12 Native Instruments Maschine

19. Reason and FL Studio are also popular sequencers. How does each of them work?

20. Maschine, the MPC, and the Korg padKONTROL are examples of what? *(See Figure 2.12)*

Figure 2.13 DJ controller system

21. Name the software package, originally released in 2000, that revolutionized DJing and allowed DJs to mix, scratch, sample, and beat-match MP3s. *(See Figure 2.13)*

Figure 2.2 First instrument with mechanical gears

Figure 2.3 Device that transmits Morse code

Figure 2.4 Piano from 1885

Figure 2.5 A professional thereminist

Figure 2.6 Classic Minimoog

ANSWERS / STUDY GUIDE

6

1. What type of early automatic instrument could play music without a human's touch?

   The wind chimes—3000 years ago!

7

2. What was the first instrument to use gear technology? (It was cranked.) *(See Figure 2.2)*

   The hurdy gurdy in the 1400s

8

3. What invention from 1832 could play a single audible tone using electrical current—and used those tones to communicate with Morse code? (It would later inspire electronic keyboards.) *(See Figure 2.3)*

   The telegraph

16

4. What machine, invented in the late 1800s, allowed users to listen to any song at any time by loading rolls of paper into it? *(See Figure 2.4)*

   The player piano

17

5. What instrument created in the early 1900s could play *any* kind of music?

   The radio

18a

6a. Why is the theremin (from 1920) so unusual?

   It doesn't have to be touched at all to play.

18b

6b. What do each of the two metal bars on the theremin control?*(See Figure 2.5)*

   One controls pitch (notes), and the other controls volume.

7. In 1964, Bob Moog invented the first electricity-driven keyboard. It was like hooking up telegraphs in a row: low voltage = low notes and high voltage = high notes. *(See Figure 2.6)*

21a

a. In 1971, a portable version of this keyboard was made. What was it called?

   The Minimoog

21b

b. How is it still relevant?

   It is still used in many hip-hop and dance hits.

21c

c. Name two artists that use it to make music.

   Lil Jon, the Black Eyed Peas, Snoop Dogg, Jay-Z, Madonna, Britney Spears, G-Unit, Christina Aguilera, and more

Figure 2.7 Fairlight CMI

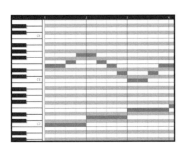

Figure 2.8 Piano roll of Beethoven's
Ode to Joy

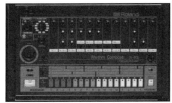

Figure 2.9 Roland TR-808

Figure 2.10 Pro Tools in a
professional studio

13   8. Name two things that were special about 1979's Fairlight
CMI.

It was the first digital sampling synthesizer.
It had a computer screen.
It could record any sound with a mic and play it back.
It had a touch screen with a light pen.

14   9. Name two artists that paid $20,000 for the Fairlight CMI.
(See Figure 2.7)

Duran Duran, Stevie Wonder, Peter Gabriel, U2, Prince, David
Bowie, Michael Jackson, Madonna, and Queen

1   10. Musical Instrument Digital Interface (MIDI) was invented in
the 1980s. What did it do? *(See Figure 2.8)*

It let musical instruments connect and play with each other (like
an early version of USB).

2   11. Where is MIDI used besides music?

Theatre lighting, video games (Rock Band, Guitar Hero, and DJ
Hero), video and audio syncing in movies, Disney robots

3   12. What is a sequencer?

Hardware or software that creates, manages, and plays music in a
particular order

4a   13a. What type of Roland drum sequencer was used in old-
school hip-hop/dance music? *(See Figure 2.9)*

The Roland TR-808

4b   13b. Who uses it to make music—and even named an album
after it?

Beyonce, Jay-Z, Sublime, Public Enemy, Britney Spears, Outkast,
Lil Wayne, the Black Eyed Peas, and Kanye West, whose album
808s & Heartbreak used the 808 extensively.

5a   14a. What kind of sequencer is Avid's Pro Tools?

Digital—it's the number-one digital audio workstation (DAW).

5b   14b. What is it used for?

Most of today's hits (any style) are recorded on it.

9   15. What could Pro Tools be compared to in the writing world?
The art world? *(See Figure 2.10)*

Microsoft Word and Adobe Photoshop

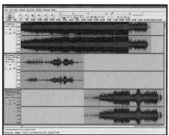

Figure 2.11 Audacity screenshot

16. How does a digital sequencer like Pro Tools give musicians total control over a song?

Artists can fix mistakes, change notes, add effects, record hundreds of tracks, and more.

17. Name one other popular sequencer.

GarageBand, ACID, Mixcraft, Logic, REAPER, and Audition

18. Name a free sequencer you can get online. *(See Figure 2.11)*

Audacity

Figure 2.12 Native Instruments Maschine

19. Reason and FL Studio are also popular sequencers. How does each of them work?

FL Studio lets you create, edit, and arrange loops of music (better for beginners). Reason is a virtual studio where you can build cool sounds, effects, and songs from scratch (for experienced users).

20. Maschine, the MPC, and the Korg padKONTROL are examples of what? *(See Figure 2.12)*

Pad controllers

Figure 2.13 DJ controller system

21. Name the software package, originally released in 2000, that revolutionized DJing and allowed DJs to mix, scratch, sample, and beat-match MP3s. *(See Figure 2.13)*

Traktor Scratch Pro

UNIT PROJECT 1

YOUR MISSION

Write a one-minute song using old-school Roland TR-808-, 909-, or 303-style sequencers, as well as some other fun audio goodies.

Resource

www.audiotool.com

Step 1: Program the Patterns

1. Go to www.audiotool.com. Create a login and password so you can save and share your work. In a classroom setting, a single login can be created for the whole class, songs can bear the names of their student creators, and all work can be saved in a central location. If you're new to this website click on Tour to learn the basics.

2. Use the Beatbox 8 (TR-808) or Beatbox 9 (TR-909).

3. Program a pattern that sounds good and makes rhythmic sense.

4. Build four drum patterns. (Use the pattern dial to select between your four patterns labelled as A1, A2, A3, and A4.)

Step 2: Sequence the Four Patterns

1. At the bottom of the editing window, click Add Track, then Beatbox 8 (or 9), and then Pattern Track.

2. Double-click inside the Timeline window to create one cycle of that pattern.

3. To change patterns, right-click the pattern, select Switch Pattern, and choose which one you'd like.

4. Input your patterns in this order:
   - A1 (Measures 1–4)
   - A2 (Measures 5–8)
   - A1 (Measures 9–12)
   - A3 (Measures 13–16)
   - A1 (Measures 17–20)
   - A4 (Measures 21–24)
   - A1 (Measures 25–28)

Step 3: Add a Music Module

1. Add either Bassline or Tonematrix to your desktop and create a musical pattern.

2. When it's ready to be added to the song, click Add Track in the editing window, then Bassline (or Tonematrix), and then Pattern Track.

3. Double-click inside the Timeline window to create one cycle of that pattern.

4. Have this pattern play *only* during the A1 sections of the song.

Grading

40 points ....Build four patterns (drums—10 points each)

10 points ....Add Bassline or Tonematrix

25 points ....Sequence patterns correctly (3.5 pts. each for A1–A2–A1–A3–A1–A4–A1)

25 points ....Effort/creativity/focus (see rubric and evaluate yourself)

100 points ....*Totally awesome!*

Effort/Creativity/Focus Grading Rubric

0–5 points ....I did just about nothing and put forth extremely low effort.

6–10 points ....I did a little more than the minimum and put forth just a little effort.

11–15 points ......I worked with average creativity and put forth average effort.

16–20 points ......I did great work, had great focus, and put forth great effort.

21–25 points ......I did top-notch work, had superior creativity, and put forth excellent effort.

Extra Credit for Your First Song

+10 points ....Use any second "synth"

+10 points ....Create additional patterns on a music module (+10 per pattern)

+20 points ....Add vocals/lyrics

+10 points ....Use any effects unit

+10 points ....Use any samples located in the sample menu

Extra Songs

You may create extra one-minute songs for up to 50 points each!

+10 points ....Use a different "synth"

+10 points ....Use a different "drum"

+10 points ....Use a different setup

+10 points ....Add vocals/lyrics

+10 points ....Use any effects unit

UNIT PROJECT 2

YOUR MISSION

Explore the world of analog synthesizers through www.synthesizers.com, the site of a company that makes old-school analog synthesizers (similar to the Minimoog) and sells them to the public. They are all made individually to what the customer needs and can afford.

Resource

www.synthesizers.com

Answer the questions below about the site on a separate sheet of paper. Click on the "Learn" menu and then go to the Beginner's Tutorial, which will help explain various synth parts.

The following navigation sections are located in a menu on the left side of the webpage:

1. **Systems.** What are the main differences among the various types of systems? List them and give examples of what some systems include.
2. **Modules.** Select four different modules and list them. Read the detailed descriptions about each link and summarize how each operates.
3. **Controllers.** Name two types of controllers. Read the descriptions for each and summarize their usage and patch tips.
4. **Cabinets /Parts.** What are four options for cabinets?

The following navigation sections are located in the menu on the top of the webpage:

5. **FAQ.** Summarize the answers to four FAQs (frequently asked questions). Choose one from each of five topic headings (Ordering, Compatibility, Company, and so on).
6. **Technical.** Name two elements of the company's design philosophy.
7. **About.** Look at the owner's personal webpage. What else does he build? What do his other companies do /sell?
8. **Artists.** Choose two artists and read their bios. Write a short summary about their music /work.
9. **Order.** How much are complete systems? What are the most and least expensive expensive parts of a synthesizer?
10. **SynthInvent.** What is SynthInvent? What is the purpose of using it?
11. **Links.** Check out Links listed for other websites. List three you found.
12. **Beginners Tutorial.** Name five facts you learned from this section.

Grading

96 points ....Each question for 1–12 (8 points each)

4 points ....Write a short reflection on what you think about this site

100 points ....*Totally awesome!*

UNIT PROJECT 3

YOUR MISSION

Make music with four awesome online sequencers and record your music with Mixcraft, GarageBand, or Audacity!

Resource 1: The Monkey

http://www.rinki.net/pekka/monkey/#

1. Program a pattern that sounds good and makes rhythmic sense.

2. Use File > Export Beat from Text and copy /paste your beat into a Word file. This way you can save your beat and upload it using File > Import Beat from Text later.

3. Save the Word file in your personal folder.

Resource 2: 909 Drum Emulator

http://lab.andre-michelle.com/fl-909

1. Use Ctrl+ or Ctrl- to zoom in or out to see the interface more easily.

2. Program a song consisting of four original drum patterns.

3. Play back and record the song using Mixcraft, GarageBand, or Audacity. (See how in the "Audacity Quick Start" section.)

4. Save your WAV file in your personal folder.

Resource 3: Fatboy Slim Sequencer (Dance Music)

www.bbc.co.uk/radio1/fbs/intro.htm

1. Program a song that lasts the length of the blocks. It must have repeating patterns.

2. Play back the song and record it using Mixcraft, GarageBand, or Audacity.

3. Save your WAV file in your personal folder.

Resource 4: Bruce Lee Sequencer / Remixer

http://www.skop.com/brucelee/index.htm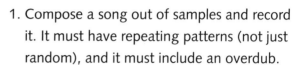

1. Compose a song out of samples and record it. It must have repeating patterns (not just random), and it must include an overdub.

2. Play back the song and record it using Mixcraft, GarageBand, or Audacity.

Grading

25 points ....The Monkey

25 points ....909 Drum Emulator

25 points ....Fatboy Slim Sequencer

25 points ....Bruce Lee Sequencer / Remixer

_____

100 points ....*Totally awesome!*

Points are granted based on creativity, musicality, and listenability of the examples.

Extra Credit for Fun (When You Finish Your Work)

BBC SOUND KIT—FUN WITH SOUND EFFECTS

http://www.bbc.co.uk/arts/multimedia/ soundkit2/

• Artfully program a song that sounds good to listen to.

• +25 points

BPOEM SOUND EFFECTS SEQUENCER (A LITTLE ODD)

http://jlapotre.free.fr/bpoem/bpoem.html

• Artfully program a song that sounds good and makes rhythmic sense.

• +25 points

THE SODAH

http://sequencer.sodah.de/ ✓

- Program a pattern that sounds good and makes rhythmic sense.
- +25 points

THE ZEFRANK

http://www.zefrank.com/sequencer

- Program a pattern that sounds good and makes rhythmic sense.
- +25 points

✓ computer

DRUMBOT

http://www.drumbot.com/projects/sequence/ ✓

- Program a pattern that sounds good and makes rhythmic sense.
- +25 points

Try using a desktop or chromebook instead of ipads

Figure 3.1

UNIT 3
REMIXING

UNIT READING

Remixing plays a part in many aspects of our lives. It's important to understand that remixing can take place in almost any discipline—architecture, education, computer science, chemistry, and many other areas. Let's look at some examples in literature, fashion, artwork, film, and music.

REMIXING IN THE ARTS

Language and literature are often remixed. The lyrical parodies of "Weird Al" Yankovic are some of the best-known comic remixes of language in music. Knock-knock jokes have formal structure but provide endless changes of linguistic content. The cutup technique of writer William S. Burroughs, in which sentences from various sources (such as newspapers, magazines, and literary classics) were literally cut into pieces with scissors and then rearranged, enabled a new way of writing and understanding linguistic meaning.

Literature

One of the most remixed works of literature is *The Wonderful Wizard of Oz* by L. Frank Baum, which has undergone myriad transformations since its initial printing in 1900. With the addition of songs, the story became a Broadway musical in 1902, which in turn became the popular 1939 film starring Judy Garland. In 1978, it evolved into a Motown film (*The Wiz*). The story also became a comic book (1975), a video game (1993), and a Muppets movie (2005). In 1995, Gregory Maguire wrote a novel about the Wicked Witch of the West, which composer Stephen Schwartz adapted into the hit musical *Wicked*. L. Frank Baum could never have predicted how much remixing his popular work would undergo.

Fashion

Fashion is also an enormous source of remixing. Think about the varieties of fashion staples: blue jeans (stonewashed, bellbottoms, skinnies), hats (fedoras, ball caps, beanies), shoes (sneakers, oxfords, loafers), and hairstyles (mohawks, buzz cuts, pompadours). Even logo designs are subject to remixing; rapper Lil Wayne appropriated the stylized "NY" logo of the New York Yankees baseball team and transformed it into a strikingly similar "YM" logo to represent his Young Money record label.

Art

Artwork is also remixed quite a bit. Andy Warhol's *Marilyn* and *Campbell's Soup Cans* depict slight variations of color and design expressed through visual repetitions. Claes Oldenburg's enormous sculptural renditions of common objects (such as the *Free Stamp)* play on the remixing of size as well as importance. In the digital realm, creating unique avatars for video games is a fun way to remix illustrated characters digitally. Finally, even guitar-body design can express wildly artistic creativity (solid-body, double-neck, sharply angled, and various colors and patterns).

Film

Videos and films are a huge source of remixing. YouTube video responses often provide a wealth of remixes based on an original viral video, easily created with software like Adobe Premiere or Sony Vegas. YouTube even offers their own downloadable free video-remixing software. *Scary Movie*, *Epic Movie*, *Vampires Suck*, and *Meet the Spartans* have remixed other films through parody. Sometimes complete remakes happen, such as filmmaker Tim Burton's 2005 remake of *Charlie and the Chocolate Factory* or his 2010 remake of *Alice in Wonderland*.

MUSIC REMIXING

There are four basic types of musical remixing: pre-recorded, tape, vinyl, and digital. Let's address these individually with examples.

Pre-Recorded

Remixing within a pre-recorded context has been happening musically for thousands of years. A key feature of tribal drumming was the improvised rhythm of individuals—they added variety to core patterns and signaled changes for singers and dancers. Baroque musicians in the 17th and 18th centuries liked to show off their improvisational abilities by adding musical ornaments like trills, turns, and grace notes to basic tunes. Transfer this style and approach to 20th-century America, and we have jazz, a genre in which no song is ever played the same way twice. In 19th-century Europe, the most familiar form of remixing occurred in the context of theme and variations; talented composers such as Ludwig van Beethoven were challenged to modify the accompaniment, chord structure, rhythm, and mood of original tunes. Additionally, some composers would incorporate familiar tunes into new works. For example, the melody of "The Star Spangled Banner" makes appearances in Giacomo Puccini's opera *Madama Butterfly*, Richard Wagner's *American Centennial March*, and Louis Moreau Gottschalk's *The Union*.

Tape

The invention of magnetic tape in the 1930s signaled a new era of musical remixing. Tape was the dominant way to record musicians in professional studios up until the late 1990s. As a result, it invited composers to splice, dice, and loop. *Musique concrète,* or music created from found recorded sounds (rather than written down), would never have been possible without tape—listen to Pierre Schaeffer's *Étude Aux Chemins De Fer* for his rhythmic collage of recorded sounds produced by steam trains. In 1956, composer Karlheinz Stockhausen blurred the lines between organic and synthetic sounds when he mixed acoustically recorded voices of children with electronic tones in *Gesang der Jünglinge*. Composer Steve Reich experimented with tape loops in many of his compositions (including *It's Gonna Rain*). The medium's pliability was also tested by pop artists like The Beatles, who used track-bouncing techniques to layer many sounds and instruments on their landmark 1967 album *Sgt. Pepper's Lonely Hearts Club Band.* Later they used tape as a means to compose sonic experiments like "Revolution 9."

Vinyl

Vinyl records were available to the general public in the late 1800s, but they were not used for remixing until the 1970s. *Hip-hop music* changed that. In the South Bronx, *DJs, or disc jockeys,* developed new techniques to play records. Hip-hop pioneer Grandmaster Flash would spin his favorite five-second drum break on one turntable, then cut to a second turntable and spin that same five seconds again on a duplicate record. Juggling back and forth, this technique (called *backspinning*) created an endless groove over which *emcees,* hip-hop vocalists, could rap and breakdancers could battle. DJ Grand Wizzard Theodore's invention of the scratch gave DJs an opportunity to rhythmically create new sounds and melodies from bite-sized pieces of recorded material. It was incredibly exciting to hear old songs become entirely new through vinyl remixing.

Digital

We are currently living in the era of digital remixing. Powerful new software (like Avid Pro Tools and Ableton Live) and hardware (such as Akai's APC/MPC or Korg's Kaoss Pad) have enabled studio musicians to sample and remix more simply than ever before. *Digital sampling* with equipment or software,

such as Traktor Scratch Pro, can give live DJs power over every element of recorded sound, turning samples into instantly playable instruments. With these tools, popular songs are routinely remixed for various purposes—a single might become a club mix, a clean radio edit, or an instrumental. Often, samples from old hits are used in new songs: Vanilla Ice's "Ice Ice Baby" caught the ear of many non-rap fans because of its use of familiar rock samples from Queen and David Bowie's "Under Pressure." Check out *whosampled.com* to discover the origins of more than 150,000 remixed songs.

Musician/producer Greg Gillis of Girl Talk created an entire career from remixed *mashups*—the seamless and often surprising combination of two or more existing songs by playing them simultaneously. Musician Mike Tompkins has over 100 million YouTube views of his a cappella renditions of pop songs. They feature layered, mashed-up recordings of his own voice imitating every instrument part. Artists like Gillis and Tompkins use samples extensively to create derivative works, which have in turn raised many legal issues about copyright and fair use. Check out *RiP!: A Remix Manifesto*, a documentary film that explores these matters in depth.

Much can be done in an educational setting on the topic of remixing. In addition to addressing some of the points outlined in this unit, you will want to jump right in and get your hands busy on a remixing project. Mixcraft, GarageBand, ACID, Reason, Ableton Live, Pro Tools, and FL Studio can be used to teach remixing of pre-recorded loops (stems) of music.

As you have seen, remixing affects many aspects of our cultural experience. Music—whether pre-recorded, tape, vinyl, or digital—has always been a medium that invites derivative works. It is *human* to remix. How will you remix *your* life?

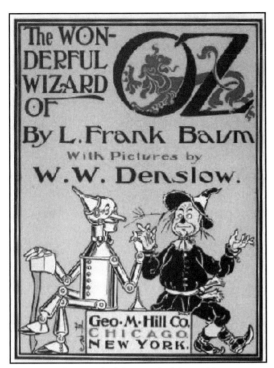
Figure 3.2 *The Wonderful Wizard of Oz, 1900*

Figure 3.3 Fashion remixing

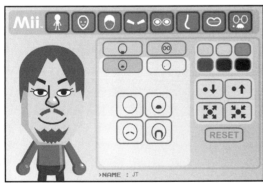
Figure 3.4 Digital artwork remixing

STUDENT WORKSHEET

1. Name five elements of creative expression / culture that can be remixed.

2. Give *two* examples of popular stories or language that have been remixed. *(See Figure 3.2)*

3. Give *two* examples of fashion remixing. *(See Figure 3.3)*

4. Give *two* examples of artwork remixing. *(See Figure 3.4)*

5. Give *two* examples of video / film remixing.

6. Give *four* types of musical remixing.

7. Give *two* examples of pre-recorded remixing. *(See Figure 3.5)*

8. Give *two* examples of tape remixing. *(See Figure 3.6)*

Figure 3.5 Pre-recorded remixing: theme and variations

Figure 3.6 Tape remixing

Figure 3.7 Vinyl remixing

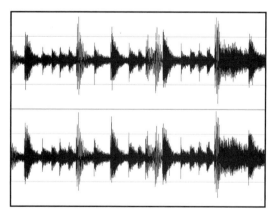

Figure 3.8 Digital remixing: break sample

9. Give *two* examples of vinyl remixing.
    (See Figure 3.7)

10. Give *two* examples of digital remixing.
    (See Figure 3.8)

11. What is a mashup?

12. Why is music remixed?

13. What are some ways you can remix music online
    for free?

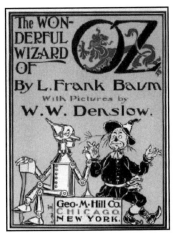

Figure 3.2 *The Wonderful Wizard of Oz,* 1900

Figure 3.3 Fashion remixing

Figure 3.4 Digital artwork remixing

Figure 3.5 Pre-recorded remixing: theme and variations

ANSWERS/STUDY GUIDE

1. Name five elements of creative expression/culture that can be remixed.

   Language, fashion, art, film, music

2. Give *two* examples of popular stories or language that have been remixed. *(See Figure 3.2)*

   The Wonderful Wizard of Oz *(The Wiz, Wicked, and so on)*
   Knock-knock jokes
   Language: saying goodbye (later, peace, deuces, bye bye), hi (yo, 'sup, howdy, hey), money (cheese, dough, bread, moolah)
   William Burroughs' cutup technique

3. Give *two* examples of fashion remixing. *(See Figure 3.3)*

   Jeans styles, shoes, hoodies, hats, book bags, tie-dye, hairstyles, Young Money logo

4. Give *two* examples of artwork remixing. *(See Figure 3.4)*

   Painting: Warhol's Marilyn *or* Campbell's Soup Cans
   Digital: Avatars, mashups, digital sampling
   Design: Guitar designs, building architecture, interior design

5. Give *two* examples of film remixing.

   David After Dentist, Scary Movie, Vampires Suck, *Tim Burton's* Charlie and the Chocolate Factory, Epic Movie, Meet the Spartans

6. Give *four* musical eras of the remix.

   Pre-recorded, tape, vinyl, digital

7. Give *two* examples of pre-recorded remixing. *(See Figure 3.5)*

   Theme and variations (such as Mozart's "Twinkle Twinkle Little Star"), interpretations of jazz tunes, Baroque ornamentation

8. Give *two* examples of tape remixing. *(See Figure 3.6)*

   The Beatles' Sgt. Pepper *album, Stockhausen's "Song of the Youth," Steve Reich's "Come Out," Pierre Schaeffer's "Train Music"*

9. Give *two* examples of vinyl remixing. *(See Figure 3.7)*

   Hip-hop, scratching

Figure 3.6 Reel-to-reel tape remixing

Figure 3.7 Vinyl remixing

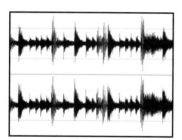

Figure 3.8 Digital remixing: break sample

10. Give *two* examples of digital remixing. *(See Figure 3.8)*

Club /radio remixes
Hardware (MPC, Maschine, TRAKTOR, any controllers)
Software (Ableton Live, Looplabs, FL Studio, anything with loops)
Mike Tompkins a cappella remixes
Greg Gillis—Girl Talk mashups
Video to music remixing (Pogo, DJ Steve Porter)

11. What is a mashup?

Blending chords and speeds of two songs into one new song

12. Why is music remixed?

To attract new listeners and give a fresh sound to old music

13. What are some ways you can remix music online for free?

mixer.pointblanklondon.com, indabamusic.com, ccmixter.org, soundation.com, jamstudio.com

UNIT PROJECT

YOUR MISSION

In this project, you will successfully create *two* one-minute remixes using music loops from the website mixer.pointblanklondon.com. You may also use the website soundation.com, as well as Mixcraft or GarageBand.

Resources
mixer.pointblanklondon.com ✓
soundation.com ✓
Mixcraft
GarageBand

If you follow these instructions carefully, you will be able to successfully create a remix. You will be making *two* remixes in *two* different music styles.

1. Go to mixer.pointblanklondon.com. Create a login and password so that you can save and share your work. In a classroom setting, the teacher can create one login for the whole class, songs can bear the names of their student creators, and all work can be saved in a central location for easy access, sharing, and assessment.

2. Choose a musical style. Any one is fine; you will be using two.

3. On the left side, select sounds by scrolling through the loop bank.

4. Listen to sounds by clicking on them.

5. Add any sound to your project window by dragging it in.

6. Toggle the loops on and off throughout the song to keep it interesting.

7. Start blending sounds! You must make a one-minute song with at least *five* different instruments.

8. When you are finished, click Save As and type your name in the Title box so you can save your work for grading.

Grading
25 points ....Use at least five loops (5 points per loop).

10 points ....Create a one-minute song (1 point per 6 seconds).

5 points ....Change either the volume or pan of any track.

10 points ....Demonstrate creativity, focus, and thoughtfulness.

50 points ....Total possible per song

You'll create two songs, worth a total of 100 points.

Extra Credit
+50 points ....Up to 50 points for each additional song you create with the same requirements

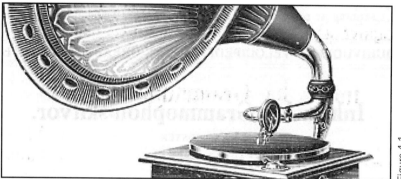

Figure 4.1

UNIT 4
Evolution of Recording Mediums

UNIT READING

Let's trace the evolution of recorded sound, which, thanks to technological advances, has gone through numerous transformations since 1860—a very short period of history. One-hundred fifty years doesn't seem like much time compared to how long humans have walked the earth. Music has been around since people could make it, but until the 1800s it was something to be enjoyed locally, in a live setting. Despite our advances within a mere 150 years of recorded sound, we are really still in the childhood years of recording. Understanding where we have been in the field of recording will help you understand where we might be able to go from here.

Early Recording

The first recording ever made was by a *phonautograph,* invented by French printer and bookseller Édouard-Léon Scott de Martinville in 1857. This recording was merely a line traced on special paper, which represented a sound. It could be studied visually but not aurally, and it could not actually be played back until computer analysis made it possible in 2008.

Edison's Cylinder

The first recording that could successfully be played back was American inventor Thomas Edison's 1878 recording of "Mary Had a Little Lamb." Edison wrapped a cylinder in tinfoil and mounted a needle on the narrow end of a cone. As he cranked the foiled cylinder around, the vibrations of his voice concentrated in the cone (acting as a microphone) and caused the needle to trace a vibrating path through the surface of the foil. Playback was achieved by cranking the cylinder, allowing the needle to retrace its path, and amplifying the vibrations back through the cone (which then acted as a speaker). Soon, Edison found that wax was a more durable solution for his recordings, and until about 1915, his wax cylinders were the iTunes of the early 20th century, and they contained only one song per cylinder.

All cylinders, also known as *records,* are played by a stylus needle, often constructed with a diamond tip that travels through a bumpy groove cut into the cylinder As it traces the groove, it is jostled around the way a bumpy dirt road might vibrate an automobile's passengers. These resulting vibrations are then amplified and played through a speaker, successfully re-creating the encoded music. Often, records are categorized according to the number of revolutions they cycle through per minute (RPM).

Gramophone Discs

Traveling at 78 RPM, flat *gramophone discs* came to replace the cylinder by the 1910s. Because they were flat, they were easier to store (conveniently stackable), and so were more space-conscious than cylinders. Recording time of these new discs varied depending upon their size. Some could hold only three to four minutes, but by the 1920s capacity allowed for eight minutes (four minutes per side)—which was significantly longer than a cylinder's playing time. From a manufacturing standpoint, flat discs were far easier to stamp with the molding machinery of the day. Additionally, manufacturers experimented with many materials to make records—ranging from rubber to shellac-based compounds. However, by the 1930s, *vinyl* would become the material of choice for producing records.

Introduced in 1948, 33 RPM discs soon came to replace the 78s, because their slower speed, larger recording area, and narrower "microgroove" allowed them to store 22 minutes of music per side. Known as *LPs* (long playing), their recording time set the standard for artists releasing albums and even continues to define the generic length of many albums released today.

In the 1950s and 1960s, 45 RPM singles (also known as 7-inch records) became very popular among rock 'n' roll fans. They had large holes in their centers to accomodate jukebox machinery.

TAPE RECORDING

Let's move away from records now and on to tape. *Reel-to-reel machines* encoded sound by arranging magnetic particles on plastic tape. The tape was wound around one reel, threaded through playback heads, and taken up by a second empty reel as it played. The earliest example of this kind of recorder was the German Magnetophon of the 1930s.

Reel-to-Reel Machines

Reel-to-reel machines became the primary way to capture new music—until the early 2000s—and were found in every recording studio. Many musicians experimented with tape in interesting ways. Musique concrète composers, such as Pierre Schaeffer, enjoyed recording sounds, cutting up the tape, rearranging the pieces, and reconnecting them in various ways. Composers such as Steve Reich experimented with repetitive tape loops, and The Beatles famously divided the tape into four narrower sections to achieve their first multitrack recordings on the album *Sgt Pepper's Lonely Hearts Club Band*. Reel-to-reel machines were also used to store information on the first computers, such as the UNIVAC.

Cassettes

Consumers were happy when small portable versions of the reel-to-reel tapes *(cassettes)* were invented. The Ford Motor Company began installing *8-track* cassette players in their cars, and cassette tapes became the dominant way to record music at home and on the go throughout the 1970s and 1980s. Cassettes were small, convenient, and easy to use, copy, and trade with friends.

Digital Media

Towards the end of the 20th century, *digital media* became the dominant format, supplanting records and tapes—which are known as analog media.

Compact Discs

Compact disc (CD) technology was invented and refined by the Philips Technology Corporation in the mid-1970s but didn't arrive on the scene for mass-market consumption until the mid-1980s. Embedded between layers of plastic in a CD is a thin aluminum layer that contains musical information. As the CD spins, a laser traces a groove embedded within the aluminum and moves from the inside of the CD toward the outside. The aluminum is etched with a series of *pits* and *lands* (high points and low points), so the laser is either reflected back off of the aluminum or absorbed into it. The resulting pattern of reflections/absorptions represents a *binary system*—ons and offs, or ones and zeroes. Whizzing by at a speed of 44,100 of these binary digits per second, our ears assemble these "samples" of sound into what we perceive as a continuous stream of music.

Apart from working differently, CDs have many advantages over tapes and records. They can be played any number of times and won't lose sound quality. CDs can also produce a wider frequency spectrum, and they are easier to store due to their compact size.

MP3s

With the rising popularity of the Internet

in the 1990s, people became interested in trading song files online, but the size of CD-quality files was prohibitively large—about 10MB (megabytes) per minute. *MP3s* were invented to reduce this file size for easier online sharing. MP3 technology effectively removes inaudible and redundant material from music, and the resulting files were so compressed that their file sizes became 10 times smaller than CD files—only about 1MB per minute. The invention of the *iPod,* Apple's portable MP3 player, in 2001 revolutionized the way people listened to music. The iPod unable users to fill thousands of songs in MP3 form onto a pocket-sized device. Physical CD collections were soon left on the shelf as listeners simply loaded their iPod with all the music they owned.

Cloud-Based Services

Another option for music storage today is the use of *cloud-based services.* Cloud-based music allows listeners to store all their music on remote servers, thereby effectively removing the need to own any physical material products. Cloud-based music is always accessible from a cell phone, a laptop, or even a remote computer with an Internet or cellular connection. Subscription services are the newest model of music consumption. Companies like Spotify, Rdio, and Beats Music have licensed and purchased millions of songs and offer their full collections to any user willing to pay a nominal fee per month (usually about $10).

The Evolution Continues

What will replace the MP3, cloud, and subscription services? Certainly the current popular format will be replaced, as it has transitioned many times over the past 150 years. Additionally, MP3s are significantly lower quality than a pure audio signal, so a change to a lossless format like *FLAC (Free Lossless Audio Codec)* is quite possible in the coming years. Perhaps one of my favorite predictions for what will replace the MP3 is the use of *DNA* to encode information. DNA's storage capacity is huge—700 terabytes in each millimeter of DNA. DNA can also be stored for long periods of time—tens of thousands of years if kept in cold, dark environments.

Here is a timeline of the evolution of musical media and when each became most popular (not necessarily when they were invented):

1860. . . . . Phonautograph

1877. . . . . Edison's tinfoil phonograph

1880s. . . . . . . Wax cylinder

1890s. . . . . . . Piano roll

1900s. . . . . . . Record disc, 78 RPM

1940s. . . . . . . Vinyl record (LP 33 RPM and single 45 RPM)

1950s. . . . . . . Reel-to-reel tape

1960s. 8-track

1970s. . . . . . . Cassette tape

1980s. . . . . . . Compact disc

1990s. MP3

1999. . . . . Napster (the first of many peer-to-peer music sharing services)

2001. . . . . iTunes

2010s. . . . . . . Music in the cloud

Figure 4.2 Édouard-Léon Scott de Martinville

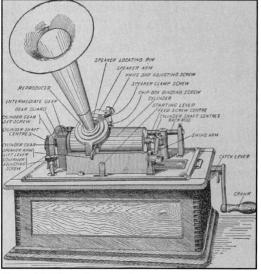

Figure 4.3 Edison phonograph

Figure 4.4 Edison cylinder, ca. 1904

Figure 4.5 Turntable cartridge and needle

STUDENT WORKSHEET

1. What is unusual about the first audio recording ever made of a human (in 1860, by Édouard-Léon Scott de Martinville)? (see Figure 4.2)

2. What was the very first song that could be played back, recorded by Thomas Edison in 1877?

3. How is music played back from a record? (see Figure 4.3)

4. How many songs could fit on a wax cylinder and how long would it play? (see Figure 4.4)

5. What is the tip of a record needle usually made of? (see Figure 4.5)

6. How many grooves are on a typical record or CD? How are they arranged?

7. What does RPM stand for?

8. Flat 78 RPM disc records replaced wax cylinders. Give two reasons why. (see Figure 4.6)

9. Why did slower and larger 33 RPM records— called LPs—come to replace 78s?

Figure 4.6 78 RPM record

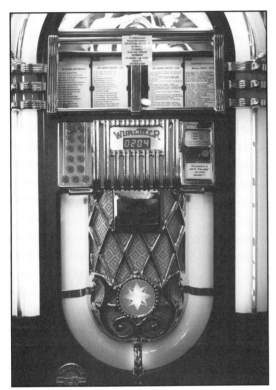

Figure 4.7 Automatic mechanical DJ

Figure 4.8 Reel-to-reel tape machine

Figure 4.9 8-track tape

10. In the 1950s and 1960s, 45 RPMs became popular with rock 'n' roll fans because they were cheap and small. What is the name of an automatic, mechanical DJ that would play these 45 RPM records one after another? *(see Figure 4.7)*

11. How do reel-to-reel machines and tape recorders encode sound? *(see Figure 4.8)*

12. What other invention of the 1950s used tape recorders to store information?

13. In the 1960s, Ford Motor Company began to encourage people to bring their favorite music on road trips by installing what in the cars? *(see Figure 4.9)*

14. What became the dominant way to record music at home in the 1970s and 1980s because it was small, convenient, and easy to use, copy, and trade with friends? *(see Figure 4.10)*

15. In the 1980s, the compact disc had several advantages. Name two. *(see Figure 4.11)*

16. What is completely different about how CDs work compared to records or tapes?

Figure 4.10 A portable mini reel-to-reel

Figure 4.11 Compact disc

Figure 4.12 iPod video, iPod Nano 2 GB, and iPod Shuffle 2 GB.

17. How do CDs play back music?

18. What specific advantage do MP3s have over CDs? *(see Figure 4.12)*

19. What is meant by "music in the cloud" and "subscription service"? Give one example.

20. What are some possible replacements for music in the cloud?

Figure 4.2 Édouard-Léon Scott de Martinville

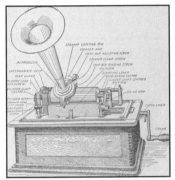

Figure 4.3 Edison phonograph

Figure 4.4 Edison cylinder, ca. 1904

Figure 4.5 Turntable cartridge and needle

Figure 4.6 78 RPM record

ANSWERS/STUDY GUIDE

1. What is unusual about the first audio recording ever made of a human (in 1860, by Édouard-Léon Scott de Martinville)? *(see Figure 4.2)*

   It could not be played back or heard until 2008!

2. What was the very first song that could be played back, recorded by Thomas Edison in 1877?

   "Mary Had a Little Lamb"—a needle on a cylinder of tinfoil

3. How is music played back from a record? *(see Figure 4.3)*

   A needle vibrates from bumps cut into the groove, then sends the vibrations to an amplifier, which makes them louder.

4. How many songs could fit on a wax cylinder and how long would it play? *(see Figure 4.4)*

   Only one song, two to four minutes long

5. What is the tip of a record needle usually made of? *(see Figure 4.5)*

   Diamond

6. How many grooves are on a typical record or CD? How are they arranged?

   Only one groove—in the shape of a spiral

7. What does RPM stand for?

   Revolutions per minute

8. Flat 78 RPM disc records replaced wax cylinders. Give two reasons why. *(see Figure 4.6)*

   They took up less space, sounded better, and had two sides, which equaled twice the music.

9. Why did slower and larger 33 RPM records—called LPs— come to replace 78s?

   They played for about 45 minutes—they were named "LP" for Long Playing.

10. In the 1950s and 1960s, 45 RPMs became popular with rock 'n' roll fans because they were cheap and small. What is the name of an automatic, mechanical DJ that would play these 45 RPM records one after another? *(see Figure 4.7)*

    The jukebox

Figure 4.7 Automatic mechanical DJ

Figure 4.8 Reel-to-reel tape machine

Figure 4.9 8-track tape

Figure 4.10 A portable mini reel-to-reel

Figure 4.11 Compact Disc

Figure 4.12 iPod video, iPod Nano 2 GB and iPod Shuffle 2 GB.

11. How do reel-to-reel machines and tape recorders encode sound? *(see Figure 4.8)*

   They arrange magnetic particles on plastic tape.

12. What other invention of the 1950s used tape recorders to store information?

   The first computers (like the UNIVAC)

13. In the 1960s, Ford Motor Company began to encourage people to bring their favorite music on road trips by installing what in the cars? *(see Figure 4.9)*

   8-track cassette tape players

14. What became the dominant way to record music at home in the 1970s and 1980s because it was small, convenient, and easy to use, copy, and trade with friends? *(see Figure 4.10)*

   The cassette tape

15. In the 1980s, the compact disc had several advantages. Name two.

   Did not lose sound quality, was easier to store than tapes (flat), lasted longer, and could play lower and higher sounds

16. What is completely different about how CDs work compared to records or tapes? *(see Figure 4.11)*

   They store digital information in binary form (zeros and ones).

17. How do CDs play back music?

   A laser is either reflected or absorbed by a series of pits and lands in the CD's aluminum layer. This generates binary data at a rate of 44,100 "pictures" of sound every second.

18. What specific advantage do MP3s have over CDs? *(see Figure 4.12)*

   They are 10 times smaller than CD files, so you can store hundreds of CDs on a tiny hard drive inside an iPod or MP3 player.

19. What is meant by "music in the cloud" and "subscription service"? Give one example.

   Internet-based storage accessible anywhere—millions of MP3s available to computers, cell phones, car radios, and so on. Users pay one monthly fee to access all the music on Spotify, Beats Music, and Rdio.

20. What are some possible replacements for music in the cloud?

   FLAC or lossless-quality files, and potentially DNA

UNIT PROJECT

—no website

YOUR MISSION

Imagine a product that will replace MP3 players, then record a 30-second radio commercial advertising it.

We have discussed how music is stored in different forms: records (information decoded on a turntable), cassettes (decoded in a tape deck), CDs (decoded in a CD player), and other types of recording technologies. The most advanced technology today are MP3s (decoded on a computer, iPod, and so on). Some consider "the cloud" to be one step beyond that!

The way we listen to and record music has evolved and changed over the last 150 years. So what comes next? What will your great-grandchildren use to record, listen to, and experience music?

For this project, you will design a new kind of recording medium and player. It must:

- Be innovative and unique.

- Have some appeal to consumers.

- Record, play, and store soundwaves (but it might also be able to record/play/store other information as well).

- Be *new*. It may *not* be a new design of an existing product. For instance, you might devise a way to encode sound in water molecules—describe how. Do not, however, design a new look for a machine that plays MP3s. You will also be writing and recording a radio commercial to market and promote your product.

QUESTIONS ABOUT YOUR INVENTION

Copy the following questions onto a separate Word document or use your own sheet of paper to answer with information about your product.

1. First, describe the medium that will store the audio information. Will it store only sound, or will it keep other information of some type as well? (For example, CD.)

2. Describe the machine that records the information onto the medium. (For example, a computer or CD pressing plant.)

3. How is the recording/storage of information achieved? How do you get new music onto your device?

4. Describe the machine/player that will decode the audio information stored on the medium. (For example, CD player.)

5. How is playback achieved? How does this player function? Be as specific/technical as necessary.

6. Give a physical description of the product, including materials, size, color, shape, and so on of your design.

7. How is your product superior to other recording mediums? What advantages are there to using your product?

8. How is your product inferior to other recording mediums? What disadvantages are there to using your product?

9. Why would anyone want to use this technology? Who will want to use it? (What is your target purchasing group?)

10. How much will each component cost?

11. Will this replace any current recording medium? Which one?

12. Provide any other helpful descriptive information.

13. Using the information from Question 3, draw/illustrate your invention. You should include a picture of both your medium and the decoding machine that "reads" the medium.

RADIO COMMERCIAL

1. Write a paragraph/script that will serve as a 30-second radio commercial about your invention that:

   - Describes your invention.
   - Explains how your invention works.
   - Convinces people to buy your invention.

Get your commercial approved before going on to Step 2!

2. Choose or even write background music to accompany the narrative. Use Mixcraft, GarageBand, or another program to record it. There are many online links for royalty-free commercial bumper music.

3. You may record the narrative with your own voice or a synthesized voice. Use Mixcraft, GarageBand, or other software to record it.

4. Blend the two in your software for a final product. Be sure to balance the voiceover and music so that it is easy to listen to and understand. You may also want to add a bit of reverb or compression to your vocals to give it a finished, professional quality.

Grading

50 points .... Questions/answers (each question is worth approximately 8 points)

50 points .... Radio commercial (each step is worth approximately 12 points)

100 points ...... *Totally awesome!*

Figure 5.1

UNIT 5
MIDI

UNIT READING

MIDI stands for Musical Instrument Digital Interface. In the late 1970s and early '80s, there were many manufacturers of electronic musical instruments, but the instruments did not have a common way to communicate with each other. A musician might own both a drum machine and a keyboard with an internal sequencer. However, the two machines would not easily be able to lock step and play together with precise rhythm. MIDI was created to solve that kind of problem, and in turn it allowed musicians to interconnect all of their musical instruments together— leading to entirely new sonic worlds created by electronics.

MIDI Communication

Developed by various music instrument manufacturer representatives in 1983, MIDI allowed machines to communicate with each other using a specialized five-pronged cable, called a *five-pin DIN*. A modern-day equivalent might be USB cables, which today act as a linking "common language" that can connect many devices together (cameras, printers, speakers, game controllers, etc.). The MIDI cable was like an early USB, but created especially for musical instruments and computers.

MIDI Instruments

Many instruments can communicate via MIDI, including keyboards, drum machines, samplers, pad controllers, digital drum pads, and wind controllers. Many MIDI instruments do not even make sounds at all, but rather trigger sampled sounds in other instruments. For example, when a musician presses a key on a MIDI keyboard controller, the keyboard sends a signal to a computer or other instrument, which accesses a bank of hundreds or even thousands of different sounds. A single MIDI keyboard could play any of those sounds, depending on which one was selected. MIDI controllers therefore became very versatile instruments.

Economy of Space

Not only did MIDI enable versatility, but it also enabled economy of space. Following its adoption, manufacturers were able to begin producing rack-mountable versions of popular keyboards. These were compact, keyless synths crammed into small boxes designed for easy portability. Suddenly, musicians no longer needed to carry multiple keyboards with them to performances—because huge sound banks and entire synth collections could be stuffed into a small suitcase, controlled with just a single master keyboard controller.

How It Works

There are basically three kinds of ports built into instruments to accommodate MIDI cables: "In," "Out," and "Thru." A musician can select a "master" instrument, and connect the "Out" port of the master to the "In" port of the "slave" instrument. With this kind of setup, the master keyboard controller can take over and play sounds (or trigger other parameters) inside the slave instrument. Connecting several instruments together using the "Thru" ports is called *daisy chaining*, which results in what's called a *layered* sound. For example, a piano sound coming from a master Yamaha keyboard could trigger flute and string sounds coming from two slave Korg keyboards; all three playing simultaneously would create a rich, layered sound. Hooking the entire setup to a computer resulted in unparalleled power to create complex arrangements and amazing music!

MIDI data can hold a lot of information about the music. It carries signals defining pitch, instrument, volume, velocity, pedaling, and also a clock signal to align everything uniformly. MIDI signals are given value on a scale of 0–127. Therefore, 128 is the maximum number of instrument sounds it can handle, as well as the maximum value for any of the aforementioned parameters. MIDI clock signals are called *MIDI time code* (or *MTC),* and are used to align multiple instruments playing together, keeping them in sync. MIDI time code is frequently used as an alignment tool by producers working to assemble sound effects and soundtracks for movies and television.

NON-MUSIC USES FOR MIDI

In addition to providing a common language for instruments, the use of MIDI coincided with the personal computing explosion of the 1980s—which allowed musicians to use computers to create professional-sounding electronic music without the need for an expensive recording studio. A device called a *MIDI interface* allows all incoming MIDI data to be recorded by a computer sequencer for modification and playback. A strong advantage to MIDI is that it is *not* an actual recording of music—it is only a set of instructions about music's parameters. This allows MIDI files to be very compact and space conservative, perfect for those early personal computers.

Computers

MIDI helped computers to "record" the musical information in layers, which could be precisely edited and arranged without the need to re-record perfect takes. MIDI allowed music to be notated in ways other than traditional notes on a staff, so it could be represented in waveforms or colorful blocks. Soon, anyone could create complex music—

even without understanding traditional notation. Removal of this literacy barrier gave amateurs great power to create music in ways never before possible.

Music Notation Software

Developed some years later, MIDI notation software programs, like Sibelius and Finale, can record music played from a keyboard (or other controller) and translate the recording into traditional staff notation. They provide a polished, clearly notated score that can easily be used for publication or use by professional musicians. Additionally, they act as a "translater" to give untrained musicians the ability to create musical scores.

Other Uses

MIDI has been used in a variety of applications. Early cell phone ringtones were created in MIDI format. MIDI is also used to control and program theatre stage lighting in a format called *MIDI Show Control*. MIDI has been used to coordinate the movements of Disney animatronic figures with music (such as in their *Pirates of the Caribbean* ride). Even the popular video games *Guitar Hero, Rock Band,* and *DJ Hero* run on MIDI, which determines if the correct notes have been "played" by the user at the proper time.

Figure 5.2 Roland TD-20 MIDI drums

Figure 5.3 MIDI cable connector

Figure 5.4 MIDI interface

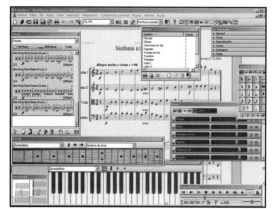

Figure 5.5 MIDI notation software

STUDENT WORKSHEET

1. What does MIDI stand for?

2. Why was MIDI invented?

3. Give three examples of MIDI instruments (also called *controllers*). *(see Figure 5.2)*

4. What can MIDI be compared to in the modern computer world?

5. Name the three types of MIDI ports on instruments.

6. What is another name for a MIDI cable? *(see Figure 5.3)*

7. What information about musical expression is transmitted over MIDI channels to tell the synths what to do? (Give three examples.)

8. What does a MIDI interface do? *(see Figure 5.4)*

9. What does a MIDI notation program do? Name a popular one. *(see Figure 5.5)*

10. Name a particular kind of everyday technology that uses MIDI.

Figure 5.6 MIDI wind controller

11. What magical MIDI number is (1) the maximum number of instruments that can be part of a bank of MIDI sounds in a synth, (2) the maximum volume they can play, and (3) the maximum number of instruments that can play at the same time? *(see Figure 5.6)*

Figure 5.7 MIDI lighting controller for theatres

12. What is MTC and what does it enable?

13. What musicians use MTC because timing is critical to their job?

14. What is a layered sound?

Figure 5.8 *Guitar Hero* game controllers

15. What is MIDI used for, apart from music? *(see Figure 5.7)*

16. What famous video games use MIDI controllers to play music? *(see Figure 5.8)*

Figure 5.2 Roland TD-20 MIDI drums

Figure 5.3 MIDI cable connector

Figure 5.4 MIDI interface

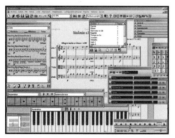

Figure 5.5 MIDI notation software

ANSWERS/STUDY GUIDE

1. What does MIDI stand for?

   Musical Instrument Digital Interface

2. Why was MIDI invented?

   So that musical instruments made by different manufacturers could "talk" to each other and control each other

3. Give three examples of MIDI instruments (also called controllers (see Figure 5.2)

   Keyboard, MIDI wind instrument, drum machine, digital drums, sampler, pad controller

4. What can MIDI be compared to in the modern computer world?

   The USB cable

5. Name the three types of MIDI ports on instruments.

   In, Out, Thru

6. What is another name for a MIDI cable? *(see Figure 5.6)*

   The five-pin DIN

7. What information about musical expression is transmitted over MIDI channels to tell the synths what to do? (Give three examples.)

   Volume, pitch (note), instrument sound, pedal information, and so on

8. What does a MIDI interface do? *(see Figure 5.4)*

   It is a small device that connects MIDI instruments to a computer for recording or editing music.

9. What does a MIDI notation program do? Name a popular one (see Figure 5.5).

   Using a controller, it can write or play back notes on a musical staff in traditional notation. Two popular ones are Sibelius and Finale.

10. Name a particular kind of everyday technology that uses MIDI.

    Cell phone ringtones

Figure 5.6 MIDI wind controller

Figure 5.7 MIDI lighting controller for theatres

Figure 5.8 *Guitar Hero* game controllers

11. What magical MIDI number is (1) the maximum number of instruments that can be part of a bank of MIDI sounds in a synth, (2) the maximum volume they can play, and (3) the maximum number of instruments that can play at the same time? *(see Figure 5.6)*

    The answer for all three is 128!

12. What is MTC and what does it enable?

    MIDI Time Code. It enables instruments to sync up rhythmically so beats are in perfect alignment.

13. What musicians use MTC because timing is critical to their job?

    Musicians who write music for TV and movies

14. What is a layered sound?

    The resulting sound when two different "instruments" on two different keyboards are triggered to play at the same time when a key is pressed (such as a flute on a Yamaha and a piano on a Korg).

15. What is MIDI used for, apart from music? *(see Figure 5.7)*

    Theatre lighting, special stage effects, VJing, controlling animatronic figures at Disney theme parks

16. What famous video games use MIDI controllers to play music? *(see Figure 5.8)*

    Rock Band, Guitar Hero, DJ Hero

UNIT PROJECT

YOUR MISSION

Make your own MIDI songs online.

Resource 1

1. Go to: http://midi.mathewvp.com/midiSequencer.htm

2. Create two MIDI songs using the online sequencer.

3. Each song must include a minimum of three drum sounds and three instruments—and should sound good when played.

4. The two songs must:

   • Be two different speeds (BPM)
   • Have two different drum beats
   • Have two different sets of instruments

5. Export the songs as MIDI files to your personal folder.

Resource 2

1. Go to: www.onlinesequencer.net

2. Create two MIDI songs using the online sequencer.

3. Each song must include four instruments and should sound good when played.

4. The two songs must:

   • Be two different speeds (BPM)
   • Have two different drum beats
   • Have two different sets of instruments

5. Export the songs as MIDI files to your personal folder.

Grading

25 points .... Website 1—Song 1

25 points .... Website 1—Song 2

25 points .... Website 2—Song 1

25 points .... Website 2—Song 2

100 points .... *Totally awesome!*

Figure 6.1

UNIT 6
THE TECHNOLOGY OF ROCK 'N' ROLL /ELECTRIC GUITARS

UNIT READING

In this unit, we'll discuss the technology of rock 'n' roll. Most importantly, this includes how electric guitars were born, how they are made, and how they function as the primary instrument in creating rock music. We'll discuss the early days of the "frying pan" guitar, the history of the Fender and Gibson companies, Les Paul's innovations, amps, types of commonly used effects pedals, and how pickups work. We'll touch on the origins of early rock 'n' roll, and how it has branched into numerous styles, including grunge, progressive rock, and heavy metal.

DEVELOPMENT OF THE GUITAR
Acoustic Guitars

First, we should talk a bit about *acoustic guitars,* which are hollow-bodied guitars that are naturally louder than electric guitars. Some forms of guitars as we know them have been around since the 1100s. Acoustic guitar strings vibrate when plucked or strummed, which in turn causes the soundboard and resonant cavity of the guitar to vibrate. Baroque-, early Romantic-, and Modern-period guitarists who play classical music on the guitar usually play a type of acoustic guitar called a *classical guitar,* which have taken on various shapes and styles over the years. Classical guitars have been played since at least the 1600s. These guitars are usually made of wood, have six nylon or catgut strings, and are played with fingernails.

Martin Steel String Acoustic

Acoustic guitars were historically a fairly soft instrument until the C.F. Martin Company introduced two innovations—the *dreadnought* design (a large, deep, square-shaped body) and steel strings. These two developments allowed the acoustic guitar to become a louder instrument.

Guitars are usually played in one of two ways—either in a flat position on the lap, called *Hawaiian style* (like country music's lap steel/slide guitars), or in a sideways position, held against the body or on the player's leg (like most folk and rock guitars).

ELECTRIC GUITARS

American inventor and musical instrument-maker George Beauchamp and craftsmen Harry Watson invented the first electric guitar, a lap-steel style instrument, in the 1930s. They nicknamed it the "frying pan" because of its appearance—resembling a frying pan! The key technology for this invention was the *pickup,* which is a magnet wrapped with wire several thousand times. The pickup, placed underneath the strings along the fingerboard, allowed the guitar sound to be transformed into electricity, which was carried into an *amplifier* to be more easily heard.

In the 1930s and 1940s, big bands were popular, playing jazz and swing music. Prior to their electrification, guitars could not be easily heard within the environment of these big bands and their huge horn sections. After being amplified, guitars could now be heard above the sounds of the horns, which allowed the guitar to flourish and begin to occupy a bit more of the limelight.

Gibson and Fender

The two major manufacturers of electric guitars, Gibson and Fender, have been competing since the 1930s. Over the past 80 years or so, these companies have taken turns advancing the technology and playability of the guitar. The Gibson ES-150 (Electric Spanish) was released to the public in 1936, at the price of $150. In 1946, American guitarist

and songwriter Les Paul invented "The Log," a one-piece, solid-body guitar made of pine wood. In addition to opening new doors for guitar players, and for the series of Gibson guitars named after him, Les Paul is well-known as an important innovator of tape machines and multitrack recording.

Fender's Telecaster (initially called Esquire) was favored by rock 'n' roll artists of the 1950s. But it was the Gibson Les Paul that really made the sound of later rock 'n' roll possible. Gibson began to experiment with different ways to amplify the guitar, and they found that when they amplified it above the normally tolerable limit, it created a bold, exciting sound. This effect was called *distortion*, and it eventually became the signature sound of rock music, and later heavy metal.

INFLUENCE OF ROCK 'N' ROLL

Rock 'n' roll was a hybrid of a few genres, notably blues/R&B, and country and western music. The first mainstream artist to successfully blend these styles in this new genre called rock was Elvis Presley, the "king of rock 'n' roll." However, Chuck Berry, a colleague and influence of Elvis, was a major architect of the rock 'n' roll style through several notable characteristics in his playing. Berry brought the guitar into the forefront by performing crazy guitar solos. His performances also had quite a bit of flair, and he became well-known for his dancing style, fast and exciting songs, and lyrics centering on teen life.

Electric Guitar Features

As guitars developed, more and more features were incorporated into their designs that would change the sound of the instrument and let guitarists create new original sounds. For example, the *whammy bar* tightens and loosens strings for special "bend" effects. *Tone knobs* control the brightness of the sound. Finally, guitarists achieve different sound qualities by switching from one set of pickups to another using a *pickup selector switch.*

External Effects

Many external types of effects boxes and pedals were also invented to change the sound of the guitar prior to amplification. *Reverb* is a popular guitar effect that imitates the echo of a large room. *Wah-wah* pedals change the sound to mimic the human voice. Other popular types of effects are *chorus, delay, phasing, looping,* and many other sound-processing types.

Innovators

As the technology of the guitar continued to evolve, talented players developed and expanded the instrument's limits and abilities. Artists such as Buddy Guy, Chuck Berry, Jimmy Page, Jimi Hendrix, Eddie Van Halen, and Eric Clapton have been some of the most popular guitarists. *Virtuosos* (musicians with extraordinarily high technical ability), like Swedish guitarist Yngwie Malmsteen, have elevated the instrument's status by bringing classical training to a decidedly modern instrument. Malmsteen is known for performing live with a full orchestra. Guitarist Michael Angelo Batio is known for extreme speed and performing on double- and even quad-necked guitars. Guitar legend Jimi Hendrix experimented with unusual tones, colors, and effects in his music. His performance of "The Star-Spangled Banner" at the 1969 Woodstock Music and Arts Festival was particularly notable; he used the guitar to imitate the sounds of war (such as bombing, guns, and screams) in a tribute to American armed forces in Vietnam.

NEW MUSIC GENRES

In the early 1970s, rock 'n' roll began to break off into many new genres. One style, *heavy metal,* featured a thick, loud sound; lots of distortion; long guitar solos; strong beats; and lyrics about aggression and masculinity. Originators of this style are the bands Black Sabbath, Judas Priest, Motörhead, Iron Maiden, and Led Zeppelin. Eventually, heavy metal transformed into *hair metal,* which became popular in the 1980s.

Punk Rock

In the mid-1970s, another new rock music genre broke out in New York City and London, England—where bands played fast, hard-edged music, short songs, politically charged lyrics, all with a strong DIY (Do It Yourself) ethic. This was *punk rock.* Groups such as The Ramones, The Sex Pistols, Crass, and The Clash rebelled against mainstream society, and their attitudes and wild fashion styles made quite a statement.

Grunge

In the 1990s, a genre called *grunge* broke out from Washington state and impacted mainstream music. It featured heavy distortion, "growling" vocals, and lyrics about frustration, all performed with a "grungy" attitude and style. Grunge included artists such as Nirvana, Soundgarden, Alice in Chains, and Pearl Jam.

Other Rock Subgenres

Over the years, literally hundreds of subgenres of rock have developed. *Speed / thrash metal* artists such as Slayer and Anthrax played extremely fast tempos and complex riffs. If you down-tune the guitar to a lower set of notes and play them slowly with intensity, you get the *doom metal* of artists like Saint Vitus and Candlemass. The use of unusual time signatures and virtuosic passages might indicate *progressive rock,* played by such bands as Yes and Rush. Additional rock subgenres include *surf rock, glam metal, southern rock, emo, death metal, black metal, grind, goth, mathcore,* and more. These subgenres are important because they have helped rock to reach new audiences.

Music made with guitars has become mainstream (rock 'n' roll), and thus the guitar has become a very popular instrument to learn. Even those who cannot play guitar love to emulate playing, such as through video games. *Guitar Hero* and *Rock Band* have become extremely popular games, allowing players to simulate playing guitar or *bass* (low-pitched instrument with four strings that looks like a guitar) in popular songs.

OTHER ELECTRONIC INSTRUMENTS

In addition to the conventional guitar, there have been some unusual experiments in similar electronic instruments in the last few decades. For example, in the late 1970s, a hybrid instrument called the *keytar* blended the guitar neck with keyboard keys. It enjoyed some popularity for a short while in the 1980s, but it has since fallen into novelty status.

In the 1980s, the first guitar MIDI controller, called the *SynthAxe,* was created. This allowed a user to plug the guitar into a computer and trigger *any* kind of sound located in the computer's sample bank—so the guitar might end up imitating a flute, a trumpet, a piano, or any other instrument.

Very recently, Moog Music (the company originally founded by Bob Moog) developed the *Moog guitar,* which is an infinitely sustaining guitar. Once strummed, the strings will resonate forever. Finally, the *Misa Kitara,* a fully digital guitar released in 2011, doesn't even have strings and allows players to interact with the instrument via fret-based push buttons and a touchscreen!

Figure 6.2 Acoustic guitar

Figure 6.3 Magnetic pickup

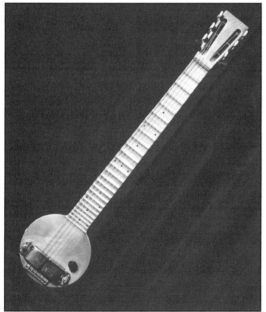

Figure 6.4 The first electric guitar

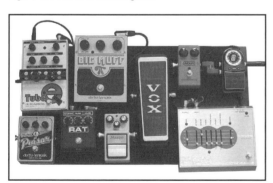

Figure 6.5 Pedalboard with effects

Figure 6.6 Les Paul, ca. 1947

STUDENT WORKSHEET

1. Which type of hollow-body guitar is naturally loud and has been around since the 1100s?
   (see Figure 6.2)

2. What is a pickup and what does it do?
   (see Figure 6.3)

3. George Beauchamp and Harry Watson invented the first electric guitar in the 1930s. What was it called? *(see Figure 6.4)*

4. Why were guitars made electric during the big band / swing / jazz era of the 1930s?

5a. What do guitar effects pedals do?
    (see Figure 6.5)

5b. What effect makes a guitar sound as if it's being played inside a large room with an echo?

5c. What effect makes a guitar sound amplified way above the limit and is heard in rock music?

6. What two major manufacturers of electric guitars have been competing since the 1930s?

7a. In 1946, Les Paul invented a solid-body guitar made of one piece of pine wood. What was it called? *(see Figure 6.6)*

7b. Why was this guitar (and its later version, called the *Gibson Les Paul*) so important?

7c. What other inventions did Les Paul help pioneer?

Figure 6.7 Chuck Berry, 1971

Figure 6.8 Velvet Elvis Presley painting

Figure 6.9 Jimi Hendrix, 1967

Figure 6.10 Heavy metal sign of the horns

8. Chuck Berry was a famous Gibson guitarist. How did he help invent rock 'n' roll? *(see Figure 6.7)*

9. Who successfully mixed rhythm and blues music with country and western music, and was the first major star of the 1950s playing this new genre called rock 'n' roll? *(see Figure 6.8)*

10. By the 1960s, rock 'n' roll was everywhere. Some guitarists, such as Jimi Hendrix, sought to break new ground with their music. What was so important about Jimi's 1969 performance of "The Star-Spangled Banner" at Woodstock Music and Arts Festival? *(see Figure 6.9)*

11. In the early 1970s, rock 'n' roll began to break off into many new genres. One style had a thick, loud sound with lots of distortion, long guitar solos, strong beats, and lyrics about aggression and masculinity. What was this and who are some of its originators? *(see Figure 6.10)*

12. In the mid-1970s, another new genre broke out in both New York City and London. Bands in this genre created fast, hard-edged music, short songs, and often political lyrics with a DIY ethic. What was this and who are some of its originators? *(see Figure 6.11)*

13. In the 1990s, a genre broke out from Washington state and impacted mainstream music. It featured heavy distortion, "growling" vocals, lyrics about frustration, and played with an aggressive style. What was this and who are some of its originators? *(see Figure 6.12)*

Figure 6.11 Punk fashionistas

Figure 6.12 Dr. Martens boots: grunge footwear

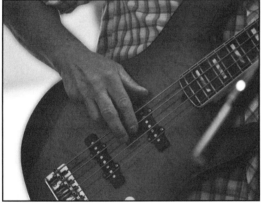

Figure 6.13 The Bass Man

Figure 6.14 Korg RK-100 keytar

Figure 6.15 Gibson Les Paul

14. Hundreds of subgenres of rock have developed, including surf rock, glam metal, progressive rock, southern rock, emo, death metal, black metal, thrash, grind, goth, mathcore, and more. Why are these subgenres important to the development of rock?

15. What are guitarists such as Yngwie Malmsteen and Michael Angelo Batio known for?

16. What instrument looks like a guitar but has only four large strings and plays low notes? *(see Figure 6.13)*

17. What instrument looks like a keyboard but is held like a guitar? *(see Figure 6.14)*

18. What's so special about the Misa Kitara digital guitar?

19. Please label this electric guitar: *(see Figure 6.15)*

- Strings
- Tuning pegs
- Fingerboard and frets
- Pickup
- Output jack
- Tone controls

Figure 6.2 Acoustic guitar

Figure 6.3 Magnetic pickup

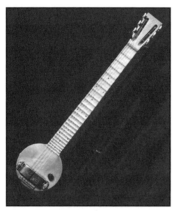

Figure 6.4 The first electric guitar

Figure 6.5 Pedalboard with effects

Figure 6.6 Les Paul, ca. 1947

Answers / Study Guide

1. Which type of hollow-body guitar is naturally loud and has been around since the 1100s? *(see Figure 6.2)*

   Acoustic guitar

2. What is a pickup and what does it do? *(see Figure 6.3)*

   It's a magnet wrapped with wire several thousand times. It changes the sound of the guitar into electricity.

3. Beauchamp and Watson invented the first electric guitar in the 1930s. What was it called? *(see Figure 6.4)*

   The frying pan

4. Why were guitars made electric during the big band/swing/jazz era of the 1930s?

   So the guitar could be heard in a large band of horns

5a. What do guitar effects pedals do? *(see Figure 6.5)*

   They change the sound of the guitar to let guitarists create new, original sounds. (See www.buzzfox.com and watch videos of effects pedals.)

5b. What effect makes a guitar sound as if it is being played inside a large room with an echo?

   Reverb

5c. What effect makes a guitar sound amplified way above the limit and is heard in rock music?

   Distortion

6. What two major manufacturers of electric guitars have been competing since the 1930s?

   Gibson and Fender

7a. In 1946, Les Paul invented a solid-body guitar made of one piece of pine wood. What was it called? *(see Figure 6.6)*

   The log

7b. Why was this guitar (and its later version, called the *Gibson Les Paul*) so important?

   It made the sound of rock 'n' roll possible.

7c. What other inventions did Les Paul help pioneer?

   Tape machines and multitrack recording

Figure 6.7 Chuck Berry, 1971

Figure 6.8 Velvet Elvis Presley
painting

Figure 6.9 Jimi Hendrix, 1967

Figure 6.10 Heavy metal sign of the
horns

Figure 6.11 Punk fashionistas

8. Chuck Berry was a famous Gibson guitarist. How did he help invent rock 'n' roll? *(see Figure 6.7)*

   He used guitar solos, was a show-off entertainer, wrote lyrics about teen life, and made fast and exciting music.

9. Who successfully mixed rhythm and blues music with country and western music, and was the first major star of the 1950s playing this new genre called rock 'n' roll? *(see Figure 6.8)*

   Elvis Presley, the "King of Rock 'n' roll"

10. By the 1960s, rock 'n' roll was everywhere. Some guitarists, such as Jimi Hendrix, sought to break new ground with their music. What was so important about Jimi's 1969 performance of "The Star-Spangled Banner" at Woodstock Music and Arts Festival? *(see Figure 6.9)*

    It was dedicated to troops in Vietnam. He made the guitar imitate sounds of war, and he used lots of feedback.

11. In the early 1970s, rock 'n' roll began to break off into many new genres. One style had a thick, loud sound with lots of distortion, long guitar solos, strong beats, and lyrics about aggression and masculinity. What was this and who are some of its originators? *(see Figure 6.10)*

    Heavy metal—Led Zeppelin, Black Sabbath, Judas Priest, Iron Maiden, Motörhead

12. In the mid-1970s, another new genre broke out in both New York City and London. Bands in this genre created fast, hard-edged music, short songs, and often political lyrics with a DIY ethic. What was this and who are some of its originators? *(see Figure 6.11)*

    Punk rock—the Ramones, the Sex Pistols, the Clash

13. In the 1990s, a genre broke out from Washington state and impacted mainstream music. It featured heavy distortion, "growling" vocals, lyrics about frustration, and played with an aggressive style. What was this and who are some of its originators?

    Grunge—Nirvana, Soundgarden, Alice in Chains, Pearl Jam

14. Hundreds of subgenres of rock have developed, including surf rock, glam metal, progressive rock, southern rock, emo, death metal, black metal, thrash, grind, goth, mathcore, and more. Why are these subgenres important to the development of rock?

    They can appeal to people from different ages and backgrounds.

Figure 6.12 Dr. Martens boots: grunge footwear

Figure 6.13 The Bass Man

Figure 6.14 Korg RK-100 keytar

15. What are guitarists such as Yngwie Malmsteen and Michael Angelo Batio known for?

    They are virtuosos—experts at technical ability and talent.

16. What instrument looks like a guitar but has only four large strings and plays low notes? *(see Figure 6.13)*

    Bass guitar

17. What instrument looks like a keyboard but is held like a guitar? *(see Figure 6.14)*

    The keytar

18. What's so special about the Misa Kitara digital guitar?

    It is played through a touchscreen and can play any kind of sound.

19. Please labcl this electric guitar: *(see Figure 6.15)*

    Strings
    Tuning Pegs
    Fingerboard and frets
    Pickup
    Output Jack
    Tone Controls

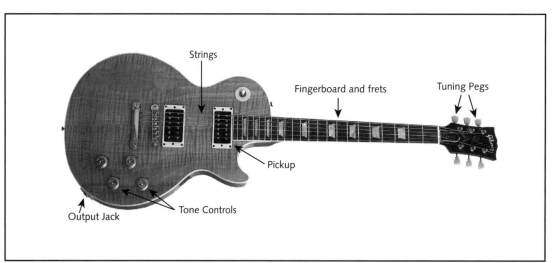

Figure 6.15 Gibson Les Paul

UNIT PROJECT

YOUR MISSION

Learn about amazing guitarists from many genres. Read, watch, write, learn, and share!

Section One

1. Go to www.digitaldreamdoor.com/pages/best_guitar-all.html.

2. Locate the names of five guitarists. Three can be names you recognize; two must be names you do *not* recognize.

3. Research the guitarists on the Internet, doing brief searches about the artists.

4. Write down three simple facts about each guitarist's playing *only* (no biographical facts). Stick to what the guitarist is known for or how the guitarist has advanced the artistry of guitar playing. Do *not* include information like place of birth or record sales. These facts can be in list form.

EXAMPLE: YNGWIE MALMSTEEN

• Famous for showmanship, elaborate solos, and pyrotechnics at his shows

• Invented the "shred guitar" style, which makes the music sound much faster

• Known for incredible virtuosity and classically oriented playing

Section Two

1. Choose one guitarist you find particularly interesting.

2. Write a short biography and background about the guitarist (three to five paragraphs or one page).

3. Discuss the guitarist's musical releases /albums, bands, songs, and so on that give credit to the artist's talent.

4. Include three reasons why the guitarist should be recognized as a great guitarist.

EXAMPLE: JERRY GARCIA

Jerry Garcia was part of the band the Grateful Dead. He was the media manager and spokesperson for the band, making him well-known to the public. During his three-decade career, he never changed styles of playing. His style was commonly regarded as "long and soulful," and because he was the lead vocalist, he also wrote many of the songs. He was known for being a great improviser and could extend a solo to great lengths. Often, the guitar solo would be the longest section of a Grateful Dead song.

Some of the Grateful Dead's albums that were released while Jerry was fronting the band include *American Beauty*, *Live /Dead*, and *Skull & Roses*. Jerry broke away from the Grateful Dead later on and created the Jerry Garcia Band, a solo project.

In 1995, he died while on tour, which only helped the Grateful Dead sell more albums, thus making him even more popular. His death sparked a renewed interest in his music and made him highly regarded as one of the best soul /rock guitarists ever.

Grading

50 points ....Section One

50 points ....Section Two

_____

100 points ....*Totally awesome!*

membrane inside it that vibrates in *sympathy* with soundwaves bumping into it. There are many types of microphones. Some basic types include *handheld, lavalier* (which can be clipped onto a lapel or collar), *headset* (useful onstage so that a singer can dance and move hands-free), *boom* (a large fuzzy mic that is held above the heads of people appearing on television and movies), and *wireless* (which can be any of the aforementioned types). Other specific types of mics exist, including *carbon, dynamic,* and *ribbon.*

Two popular microphones used for live sound applications are the Shure SM57 and SM58. These mics sound great and are extremely rugged—they are constructed durably to withstand use night after night. The membrane, *electrical transducer,* and wiring are protected by a small, strong steel-mesh cage lined with foam. This foam, called a *windscreen,* protects the microphone from rough contact, saliva, drops, and so on.

Mixer

A *mixer's* primary job is to blend multiple incoming microphone signals into a single output and to give control over those signals—a mixer can manage volume, equalization, routing, and other aspects of incoming sound. A *mixing console* has knobs to control *equalization* (treble /bass), *effects* (reverb, delay, etc.), *pan* (left versus right speakers), *monitor sends* (special speakers located onstage for performers to hear themselves), and *mic sensitivity* (how "hot" the mic is). Also, a mixer usually has a row of white sliders, known as *faders,* which control the overall volume and blending of the mics and instruments.

Sound Engineer

The person in charge of the mixer is called an *engineer,* although in live settings, that person might be called a *front-of-house engineer* or a monitor engineer. The engineer is responsible for balancing all incoming sounds, making the necessary adjustments, and making the musicians sound great!

Amplifier

An *amplifier's* primary job is to increase the power of an electrical signal. The signal, on its way from the mixer to the speakers, is given a sharp "boost" by the amp. The power of this boost is determined by the number of *watts* the amp can handle. Like microphones, there are many types of amps, but in this unit we are limiting ourselves to power amplifiers used for making music louder. The more watts an amp is rated to handle, the louder it can usually make the sound. Car stereos, coming straight from the factory without modification, usually run from approximately 40 to 100 watts. Powerful home stereos might be rated from 100 to 500 watts—plenty for a living room or garage party. Small concert clubs may use thousands of watts, while large arenas or outdoor venues may pump out 10,000 watts or more.

Speakers

Often, amplifiers are used cooperatively—anywhere from two to two dozen amps might be divided to drive several kinds of speakers at once. They might be divided to power only one side of the house sound system. Also, they might be divided using a splitter called a *crossover* to do a special job, such as powering *tweeters* (speakers that reproduce only high sounds), *midranges* (speakers that reproduce sounds in the middle range of hearing), and *subwoofers* (speakers that produce the lowest audible sounds).

A speaker's primary job is to change the electrical signal back into soundwaves. The electrical signal travels through a *voice coil electromagnet* situated between the poles of a magnet, which in turn vibrates a paper cone. The cone then pushes and pulls the air in the club, automobile, hall, or room back and forth, until the vibrations reach the listeners' eardrums. The larger the cone, the lower the sounds it can produce. A special type of speaker used onstage in live concerts is the *monitor wedge*. This speaker is wedge-shaped, usually angled up toward a singer or an instrumentalist, and allows performers to hear themselves more clearly onstage. Sometimes performers prefer to use *in-ear monitors*, which fit directly inside the ear and allow for greater freedom of movement across the stage. In-ear monitors are also helpful for aligning the performance of musical groups that prefer to play along with pre-recorded tracks.

Feedback

One of the sound engineer's primary concerns is the risk of *feedback*, which is basically the usually undesirable sound of audio getting trapped in a loop within the sound system. Feedback typically happens when a mic is angled toward a speaker. The mic picks up a frequency, which runs through the system and is amplified, coming out of the speaker at a louder volume. This louder tone is then picked up by the mic again, is run through the sound system a second time, and comes out the speaker even louder than its first pass. The unwanted frequency continues to cycle until the mic is redirected. Sometimes it can be controlled by adjusting the equalizer back at the mixer.

Rack

Sound engineers often travel with quite a bit of special equipment, all loaded into a giant travel-ready durable box called a *rack*. In a rack, you might find preamps, equalizers, crossovers, effects units, compressors, and more. The use of this equipment often holds the engineer's secrets for great sound and even provides the "signature" sound some artists are known for.

Sound Check

Prior to a live evening concert, *sound checks* are held to prepare for the big night. Sound checks serve multiple purposes—to balance the sound of onstage instruments and singers, to eliminate potential feedback problems, and to ensure that the mix sounds right within the particular acoustic space. Also, if a component is missing or is not working, there's time to run to the local music store to pick up a replacement part.

Recording Booth

In a recording studio, the *booth* is a small soundproof room in which singers and instrumentalists record. It is separate from where the engineer/producer works with the mixing equipment to do the recording. Studios are designed to control sound in order to obtain the best-quality recording possible. As a result, the concrete or brick walls are usually built extra thick, join at odd angles, and are covered with sound baffling/padding. Doors are doubled and often have a pocket of air in between so that soundwaves don't enter or exit the studio.

Sound systems and recording studios are complex entities. The successful management of their practical use is both an art and a science.

Figure 7.2 Shure SM58 handheld mic

Figure 7.3 Headset mic

Figure 7.4 Lavalier mic

Figure 7.5 Boom mics

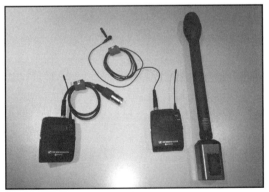

Figure 7.6.1 Sennheiser wireless system

Figure 7.6.2 Windscreen

STUDENT WORKSHEET

1. List or draw the signal chain of six basic events in sound systems.

2. What is the primary job of a microphone?

3. Name *five* different kinds of mics. *(see Figures 7.2–7.6.1)*

4. What is the purpose of the wire mesh and foamy windscreen on a microphone? *(see Figure 7.6.2)*

5. What are the Shure SM57 and SM58 renowned for?

6. What is the primary purpose of a mixing board? *(see Figure 7.7)*

7. Who is in charge of the mixer and makes a live band sound great?

8. What do some of the knobs on the mixer control? (Name three functions.) *(see Figure 7.8)*

9. What's another name for the sliders on a mixer, and what do they do? *(see Figure 7.9)*

Figure 7.7 Mackie 1402-VLZ mixer

Figure 7.8 Knobs on a mixer

Figure 7.9 Faders on a mixer

Figure 7.10 Rack of Crown amplifiers

10. What is the primary purpose of an amplifier?

11. How are amps rated? *(see Figure 7.10)*

12. List the approximate amount of wattage needed to power the following:

    a. Car stereo

    b. Powerful home stereo

    c. Small concert club

    d. Large arena / outdoor venue

13. What is a speaker's primary job? *(see Figure 7.11)*

14. What is a monitor? Name two types. *(see Figure 7.12)*

15. What is a crossover?

16. What is the purpose of a sound check?

Figure 7.11 Line array of speakers

Figure 7.12 Onstage monitor wedges

Figure 7.13 Rack of compressors and effects

Figure 7.14 Recording booth

17. What is feedback?

18. What is the name of the large, durable box that holds other "special effects" equipment the sound engineer uses (such as compressors, preamps, effects units, EQs, and so on)? (see Figure 7.13)

19. In a recording studio, what is the name of the small, soundproof room in which the singers and instrumentalists record? (It is separate from where the engineer/producer works.) (see Figure 7.14)

20. Name two ways the design of a recording studio helps to control sound for excellent recording.

Figure 7.2   Figure 7.3 Headset mic
Shure SM58
Handheld mic

Figure 7.4 Lavalier mic

Figure 7.5 Boom mics

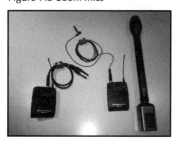

Figure 7.6.1 Sennheiser wireless
system

Figure 7.6.2 Windscreen

Figure 7.7 Mackie 1402-VLZ mixer

Figure 7.8 Knobs on a mixer

ANSWERS/STUDY GUIDE

1. List or draw the signal chain of six basic events in sound systems.

   Singer/instrument—microphone—mixer—amplifier—speaker—ear

2. What is the primary job of a microphone?

   It converts audio signals into electrical signals.

3. Name *five* different kinds of mics.

   Handheld (see Figure 7.2), lavalier (see Figure 7.4), boom (see Figure 7.5), headset (see Figure 7.3), wireless (see Figure 7.6.1)

4. What is the purpose of the wire mesh and foamy windscreen on a microphone? *(see Figure 7.6.2)*

   They protect the mic from saliva, rough contact, and strong air gusts.

5. What are the Shure SM57 and SM58 renowned for?

   They're used in live concerts around the world, and they're built like tanks.

6. What is the primary purpose of a mixing board? *(see Figure 7.7)*

   It combines all mic/line inputs into one output and controls the sound.

7. Who is in charge of the mixer and makes a live band sound great?

   The front-of-house sound engineer

8. What do some of the knobs on the mixer control? (Name three functions.) *(see Figure 7.8)*

   Treble/bass, special effects, speakers for the band (monitors), mic sensitivity, pan (left/right)

9. What's another name for the sliders on a mixer, and what do they do? *(see Figure 7.9)*

   Faders—they control volumes of the mics and instruments.

10. What is the primary purpose of an amplifier?

    To boost the electrical signal on its way to the speaker

11. How are amps rated? *(see Figure 7.10)*

    According to watts—the more watts, the louder they are

Figure 7.9 Faders on a mixer

Figure 7.10 Rack of Crown amplifiers

Figure 7.11 Line array of speakers

Figure 7.12 Onstage monitor wedges

Figure 7.13 Rack of compressors and effects

Figure 7.14 Recording booth

12. List the approximate amount of wattage needed to power the following:

a. *Car stereo: 40–100*
b. *Powerful home stereo: 100–500*
c. *Small concert club: 500–5,000*
d. *Large arena /outdoor venue: 10,000 or more*

13. What is a speaker's primary job? *(see Figure 7.11)*

It converts electrical signals to audio signals (the opposite of a mic).

14. What is a monitor? Name two types. *(see Figure 7.12)*

An onstage speaker that lets performers hear themselves play or sing.

15. What is a crossover?

A unit that directs an amplifier's power to drive specific speakers— high, midrange, or low.

16. What is the purpose of a sound check?

To balance the sound of the band, eliminate feedback, and detect problems

17. What is feedback?

When sound gets trapped in a loop and amplified into a terrible noise

18. What is the name of the large, durable box that holds other "special effects" equipment the sound engineer uses (such as compressors, preamps, effects units, EQs, and so on)? *(see Figure 7.13)*

The rack

19. In a recording studio, what is the name of the small soundproof room in which the singers and instrumentalists record? (It is separate from where the engineer /producer works.) *(see Figure 7.14)*

The booth

20. Name two ways the design of a recording studio helps to control sound for excellent recording.

Walls are not parallel, sound baffling /padding is used everywhere, walls are extra thick and often made of concrete or brick, doors are doubled and often have a pocket of air in between. Sound should not leak in or out.

UNIT PROJECT 1

YOUR MISSION

You will be provided with *multitrack stems*, individual audio files, of music from a real recording studio. It will be your job to engineer and produce the raw tracks into a finished, listenable song. First, follow the simple engineering project instructions below using different genres of music. When you are familiar with the basics, you will want to "graduate" to other mixing books to expand your skill set. Complete your project by using stem excerpts. from www.tinyurl.com/mixpractice (which is a shortened link to http://www.cambridge-mt.com/ms-mtk.htm#BlueLitMoon).

Resource

www.tinyurl.com/mixpractice

What to Do

1. The teacher will play musical tracks of different styles for 15 seconds each. You may also choose to explore the preview MP3s on the site on your own. Write down your five favorites.

2. The teacher will play the 32 tracks again for 10 seconds each. Narrow down your choices to your favorite two. You will mix only one song; save the other if you want to do extra credit (5 points). On your first try, just work with mixes that have 15 or fewer tracks. On a second or third round, you can try mixing more complex sessions.

3. The teacher will upload your favorite song to your flash drive. These will be found in a folder called Mix Practice.

4. Download either the excerpt or the full track to your computer.

When you're getting ready to mix, first locate the zip folder containing the tracks. Then:

5. Right-click the song file and choose Extract All > Extract to the same folder, which opens the little "envelope" of tracks. (5 points)

6. Open Mixcraft, GarageBand or Audacity. (5 points)

7. Drag or import all the tracks into the digital audio workstation. (5 points)

8. Organize the tracks into a logical order. (5 points)

9. Listen to every single track by itself using Solo first—for the whole song. You will be listening to the song several times. You can use Solo any time you are working on an instrument to help you hear what changes are happening. Familiarize yourself with these tracks independently before making any mixing changes. (15 points)

10. Use the volume sliders to turn up and down instruments for a good, balanced mix. (10 points)

11. Find a spot in the middle of the song to isolate one track. Remove audio using automation from all tracks but that one. Now you'll hear just one track playing.—this will sound like a "breakdown" to just one track. (5 points)

12. Do it two more times, each time with a different instrument. (10 points)

13. Use Effect > Reverse on any small portion of a track. (5 points)

14. Use Effect > Change Pitch on any small portion of a track. (5 points)

15. Use Effect > Phaser on any small portion of a track. (5 points)

16. Use any other effect of your choice on any small portion of a track. (5 points)

17. Use Master Track Fade In for all tracks at the beginning of the clip. (5 points)

18. Use Master Track Fade Out for all tracks at the end of the clip. (5 points)

19. Bleep out an imaginary swear word! These are "clean" songs already, but place a censoring tone at least one place in the song. Select the word, use Generate > Tone, and choose Frequency = 800. Alternately, you can simply "Reverse" a single word to "clean" it up. (5 points)

20. Save your final project and give your finished mix a name. (5 points)

Grading
Each question has the number of points indicated in parentheses.

Total points.........100 points

UNIT PROJECT 2

YOUR MISSION
In this project you will play the role of musician/composer as well as sound engineer. You will write a song, record the song, and engineer the mix in a highly simplified way using an online program called JamStudio.

Resource
www.jamstudio.com

What to Do
1. Go to www.jamstudio.com. Create a login and password so you can save and share your work. In a classroom setting, one login can be created for the whole class, songs can bear the names of their student creators, and all work can be saved in a central location.

2. You will create a simple blues song with a middle section in A–B–A form.

Chords in a blues song always follow a specific order. Your teacher can help you understand how to transpose to different keys. Here is your "A Section" written in the key of G Major:

G–G–G–G

C–C–G–G

D–C–G–G

3. The middle section, which you will compose on Page 2, needs totally different instruments and style. If you are writing in the key of G, use the chords from the following (your B section). If you are writing in a different key, your teacher can help you to transpose them:

Em–C–Em–C or Em–C–Am–D or G–F–C–D

4. You don't have to keep the song in the key of G, as listed above. You can change keys. Ask your teacher how to transpose the music to another key.

5. Your song needs to play in the order of A–B–A, so type "1,2,1" in the Play Page Order box. This will guarantee your song sounds great!

6. Experiment and choose any instruments or styles you'd like. Mix the instruments with care—listen to what you'd like to be louder or softer. Be original!

7. When you are finished, click on Save and title the song your full name, such as John Smith.8. You may create extra songs for extra credit in the same A–B–A format.

Grading
25 points ....Following the correct blues chords listed earlier

25 points ....Having the correct order of the song in A–B–A

25 points ....Taking care to choose a nice instrumentation with a different B section

25 points ....Demonstrating originality
and creativity

100 points ....*Totally awesome!*

Effort / Creativity / Focus Grading Rubric

0–5 points ....I did almost nothing and put
forth extremely low effort.

6–10 points ....I did a little more than the
minimum and put forth just
a little effort.

11–15 points ......I worked with average
creativity and put forth
average effort.

16–20 points ......I did great work, had great
focus, and put forth great
effort.

21–25 points ......I did top-notch work,
showed superior creativity,
and put forth excellent
effort.

Figure 8.1

UNIT 8
THE TECHNOLOGY OF HIP-HOP

UNIT READING

It's important to do some homework on *hip-hop*. To neglect studying this popular genre is to neglect the cultural world we are living in. For some, it can be challenging to push past the sometimes vulgar language and explicit imagery associated with hip-hop, but it's exceedingly important to shift viewpoints; hip-hop is a culture with credibility, substance, and intelligence that has influenced millions of people.

HIP-HOP CULTURE

Hip-hop is not just a style of music. Its scope is incredibly broad, because it encompasses an entire culture and a way of life. Any culture has its own elements, such as unique styles of music, dance, fashion, art, and language—and hip-hop is no different. The music of hip-hop is expressed through turntables, microphones, drum machines, and samplers. Emcees / rappers develop the "slanguage" of hip-hop. Graffiti artists provide a visual component to this soundtrack, while *B-boys* (breakdancers) develop athletic dance moves in the form of *breakdancing,* a style of street dancing that developed in New York City in the 1980s. The fashion of hip-hop can range from old-school Adidas to the most recently released Jordans.

Roots

Hip-hop's roots can be traced back to Jamaica in the 1950s and 1960s, with its pervasive sound-system culture. Disc jockeys (DJs) would organize large dancehall parties and events, blasting ska, reggae, and rocksteady music at the loudest possible volumes. The DJs engaged in friendly competition, both by increasing the size and power of their sound systems and by finding and playing new music. At these events, DJs would work with emcees (MCs), who were responsible for communicating with the audience, praising the DJ, and generally keeping the flow of the evening going. MCs such as U-Roy (often credited with being the first freestyle rapper) would speak in clever rhymes, either prewritten or improvised, and eventually this job function transferred to parties held in the South Bronx, New York City.

DJ Kool Herc

Clive Campbell, known as DJ Kool Herc, moved from Jamaica to the South Bronx. Influenced by the dancehall music of Jamaica, he began to DJ his own parties in his neighborhood playing ska and reggae for these get-togethers. Although disco was hitting the mainstream, audiences in the Bronx really loved hearing genres like Motown, funk, soul, and R&B. As interest grew, Kool Herc invented some skills that allowed him to keep the crowd's interest. He began to focus on the "break" of songs, which was generally a short instrumental section (usually the bridge or rhythmic breakdown) that featured the drums. Dancers loved the break, so using two turntables, Herc began to string the breaks of many songs back to back, often at the peak of the evening's party.

Grand Wizzard Theodore and Grandmaster Flash

Kool Herc became a legend and influenced many other young DJs in New York, who in turn contributed to creating new, inventive ways of entertaining their crowds. Two of those young DJs were Grand Wizzard Theodore (Theodore Livingston) and Grandmaster Flash (Joseph Saddler). Grand Wizzard Theodore is generally credited with inventing the scratch. While practicing his DJ skills in his room as a youngster, his mother told him to turn the music down or else she would make him turn it off. As she was talking

to him, he was holding the record still with his fingers, and he heard the rubbing sound of the needle on the vinyl. He experimented rhythmically with the sound and began to regularly use it purposefully in his gigs.

One of Grandmaster Flash's greatest contributions was perfecting the extension of the disco break Kool Herc had become known for. However, Grandmaster Flash is also widely known for his development of backspinning and *beatmatching* in conjunction with the *crossfader*. A crossfader is a slider on a mixer that can either isolate music from one turntable or allow the two turntables to play simultaneously. Grandmaster Flash realized that if he used two copies of the same record, he could extend the instrumental break as long as he wanted. He would cue the break on each turntable. After playing the break on turntable 1, he would slide the crossfader over and let turntable 2 play. While turntable 2 was playing, he would manually "rewind" the record on turntable 1 to cue up the break again. After turntable 2 was finished, the crossfader went back to turntable 1 again. In this way, through manual sampling of those few seconds of music, he could extend the break for as long as he saw fit.

Talented DJs would compete against each other and often embarked on a "quest" for beats without genre discrimination, seeking fresh music from unusual sources. They would play Broadway musicals, commercial and television themes, obscure blues records, early heavy metal, and Bollywood tunes. Even today, hip-hop is still full of samples from all styles of music.

Rise of the MC

Eventually, MCs, who would chatter over the DJ's extended breaks, began to eclipse the DJ's star quality. With their clever rhymes and crowd-motivation tactics, MCs refocused the limelight on themselves. Rhymes became more complex, freestyle battles increased the MCs' poetic agility, and wordplay became paramount as they battled their way to dominance of the mic.

Lyrically, hip-hop often carries double meanings/messages in the same tradition as African American spirituals. Today, some talented rappers can sustain double and triple entendres as well as extended metaphors, and use the technique of mispronounciation to blur meaning—all in a freestyle improv reminiscent of the greatest jazz players.

HIP-HOP IN THE MAINSTREAM

Although creativity flourished within all facets of hip-hop culture for several years, it remained primarily confined to New York City. It wasn't until 1979, when hip-hop pioneers The Sugarhill Gang released their catchy hit single "Rapper's Delight," that hip-hop became mainstream. "Rapper's Delight" sampled a bass line by the 1970s disco-funk band Chic and even included the words "hip-hop," giving this new genre a name that stuck.

Zulu Nation

Also around this time, New Yorker Afrika Bambaataa, a former gang member, left his gangster lifestyle and formed the hip-hop collective Zulu Nation. This group of artists, MCs, DJs, and B-boys, were anti-racist and anti-violent, and they prided themselves on becoming socially and politically aware. They chose to battle each other with the forces of creativity instead of with weapons. One of Bambaataa's most important contributions was the song "Planet Rock," recorded in 1981. This tune was unique because it introduced the use of drum machines and samplers into hip-hop—a move up the evolutionary scale of technology from the genre's traditional use of turntables.

MTV Era

Starting in the early 1980s, hip-hop was no longer the Bronx's best-kept secret, as it began to influence mainstream music. The Queens, New York hip-hop group Run-D.M.C.'s 1986 cover of rock band Aerosmith's hit "Walk This Way" is often credited with helping to break hip-hop into the mainstream—especially because it aired so often on MTV. Also that year, fellow New Yorkers the Beastie Boys' mainstream hit album *Licensed to Ill* was the first rap album to top the *Billboard* charts. For many, this was the first time hip-hop had truly made its way into homes across the country, impacting suburban families in states far away from New York.

Gangsta Rap

There was a rise of hip-hop culture on the west coast throughout the early 1980s as well, but its most significant contribution to the genre would come in the form of *gangsta rap*. Gangsta rap originated in Los Angeles, California and depicted in explicit detail the tough nature of street life, gang activity, crime, violence, and sexuality. While Ice-T's (Tracy Lauren Marrow) 1986 opus "6 in the Mornin'" is credited as a defining track of gangsta rap, NWA's 1988 album *Straight Outta Compton* established the subgenre and helped popularize it. Ice-T and NWA were based in the South Los Angeles neighborhoods of Crenshaw and Compton.

Intellectual Hip-Hop

Tupac Shakur added an intelligent spin on gangsta rap, intellectualizing the problems in his own difficult life through a lens many young blacks could relate to as he rapped about issues such as racism, poverty, and incarceration. Shakur was born in Harlem, New York but moved to northern California in his teens. New York group Public Enemy also helped make hip-hop less of a party train and more of a vehicle to educate and inform listeners about segregation, politics, and equality issues in the U.S.

Sampling in Hip-Hop

Rap music—simply defined as clever rhyming over a catchy hook—has traditionally used familiar songs or beats as source material. Vanilla Ice's "Ice Ice Baby" sampled the rock song "Under Pressure" by Queen and David Bowie, while Jay-Z's "Hard Knock Life" sampled music from the musical *Annie*. This practice of sampling has led to lawsuits and issues of copyright control. However, hip-hop continues to evolve by cross-pollinating with different kinds of samples and styles. For example, Detroit rapper Kid Rock creates country-flavored hip-hop, and Outkast from Atlanta, Georgia makes marching band- and jazz-related hip-hop. Examples like these gave hip-hop widespread appeal to a diversified listener base of many ages and backgrounds.

Hip-Hop Production

Today, many software titles aid in the production of hip-hop. FL Studio, Reason, MegaMusicMaker, DUBturbo, BTV Solo, Pro Tools, Ableton Live, Logic Pro, and SONAR are just a few. One can also modify vocals using effects processers, including one rapper T-Pain helped popularize, called *Auto-Tune*.

Many hardware solutions also exist for creating hip-hop: traditional rhythm and music machines (Roland 808s / 909s), various synthesizers (Ensoniq ASR-10, Korg TRITON, Roland Fantom, Yamaha Motif, Minimoog), pad controllers (Akai MPC series, M-Audio Trigger Finger, Korg padKONTROL, Maschine), turntable mixers, and of course the favorite DJ turntable of all time, the Technics SL-1200.

Figure 8.2 1520 Sedgwick Ave in the Bronx: site of the first hip-hop parties

Figure 8.3 Turntables and mixer

Figure 8.4 Behringer dx626 mixer

Figure 8.5 Thai breakdancers

STUDENT WORKSHEET

1. What is hip-hop?

2. What are the four basic cultural elements of hip-hop?

3. Where did hip-hop originate? *(see Figure 8.2)*

4. What does DJ stand for?

5. In the 1970s, DJ Kool Herc came to the U.S. from Jamaica and used his huge sound system to play music at parties. What *two* kinds of music from Jamaica were originally played at NYC parties and served as the original source for hip-hop music? *(see Figure 8.3)*

6. NYC audiences preferred hearing other types of music. What genres were especially popular at these parties? What genre was mainstream at that time?

7. What tool allows a DJ to control the volumes of two turntables mixed together? *(see Figure 8.4)*

8. What is beatmatching?

Figure 8.6 Grand Wizzard Theodore

Figure 8.7 Early emcee Melle Mel

Figure 8.8 Afrika Bambaataa and DJ Yutaka

Figure 8.9 Run-D.M.C. custom Adidas shoes

9. What is the break of a song? How is it used? *(see Figure 8.5)*

10. DJs also experimented with different ways to play their records. DJ Grand Wizzard Theodore invented what technique that changed how we listen to music today? *(see Figure 8.6)*

11. What does MC stand for? *(see Figure 8.7)*

12. Who was U-Roy?

13. Why was the Sugarhill Gang's 1979 album important in the history of rap music?

14. Afrika Bambaataa started an organization of positive, anti-violent, anti-racist artists, dancers, DJs, and MCs called the Zulu Nation. What was special about Afrika's song "Planet Rock?" *(see Figure 8.8)*

15. By 1986, some hip-hop became mainstream. What was unique about Run-D.M.C.'s collaboration with Aerosmith in 1986? *(see Figure 8.9)*

16. By 1986, hip-hop began to change. One group, Public Enemy (featuring Flavor Flav), wrote what kind of music? *(see Figure 8.10)*

Figure 8.10 Flavor-Flav of Public Enemy

17. By 1987–1988, artists such as NWA, Ice-T, and Geto Boys rapped about tough life on the streets, gangs, crime, and poverty. What kind of music did they invent?

18. What is the art of imitating the sound of drums and scratching with the voice?

Figure 8.11 Vintage Akai MPC60 pad controller

19. What is the competitive art of using spray paint to tag buildings, subways, and other urban areas called?

20. Many rap songs, such as Vanilla Ice's "Ice Ice Baby" and Jay-Z's "Hard Knock Life," have traditionally used familiar songs to back up their music. What is this called? *(see Figure 8.11)*

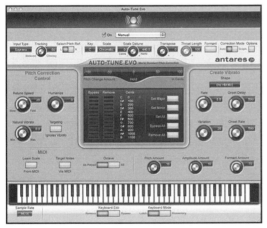

Figure 8.12 Autotune on GarageBand

21. What is a popular way to change the sound of vocals in hip-hop today? (T-Pain is known for popularizing it.) *(see Figure 8.12)*

22. This has led to combining different styles of music—for example, country (Kid Rock) and swing/jazz (Outkast). Why is this important for hip-hop's future?

Figure 8.2 1520 Sedgwick Ave in the Bronx: site of the first hip-hop parties

Figure 8.3 Turntables and mixer

Figure 8.4 Behringer dx626 mixer

Figure 8.5 Thai breakdancers

Figure 8.6 Grand Wizzard Theodore

Figure 8.7 Early Emcee Melle Mel

ANSWERS/STUDY GUIDE

1. What is hip-hop?
   It is a culture, a way of life.

2. What are the four basic cultural elements of hip-hop?
   DJing (also beatboxing, which imitates the DJ), rap (MCing), graffiti (the art of hip-hop), and dance (breakdancing and B-boying). Language (slang) and fashion are also sometimes considered.

3. Where did hip-hop originate? *(see Figure 8.2)*
   South Bronx, NYC

4. What does DJ stand for? *(see Figure 8.3)*
   Disc jockey

5. In the 1970s, DJ Kool Herc came to the U.S. from Jamaica and used his huge sound system to play music at parties. What *two* kinds of music from Jamaica were played at NYC parties and served as the original source for hip-hop music?
   Ska and reggae

6. NYC audiences preferred hearing other types of music. What genres were especially popular at these parties? What genre was mainstream at that time?
   Soul, R&B, funk, Motown. Disco was mainstream.

7. What tool allows a DJ to control the volumes of two turntables mixed together? *(see Figure 8.4)*
   A crossfader

8. What is beatmatching?
   Changing the speed of one song to match another to seamlessly play them without stopping. It keeps the dancers dancing!

9. What is the break of a song? How is it used? *(see Figure 8.5)*
   The best five seconds of a song, played over and over using two turntables. MCs and breakdancers use it to feature talents.

10. DJs also experimented with different ways to play their records. DJ Grand Wizzard Theodore invented what technique that changed how we listen to music today? *(see Figure 8.6)*
    The scratch

11. What does MC stand for? *(see Figure 8.7)*
    Master of ceremonies, or emcee

12. Who was U-Roy?
    The first freestyle rapper/MC (from Jamaica)

Figure 8.8 Afrika Bambaataa
and DJ Yutaka

Figure 8.9 Run-D.M.C. custom
Adidas shoes

Figure 8.10 Flavor-Flav of Public
Enemy

Figure 8.11 Vintage Akai
MPC60 pad controller

Figure 8.12 Autotune on
GarageBand

13. Why was the Sugarhill Gang's 1979 album important in the history of rap music?
It was the first rap music recording and included the term "hip-hop."

14. Afrika Bambaataa started an organization of positive, anti-violent, anti-racist artists, dancers, DJs, and MCs called the Zulu Nation. What was special about Afrika's song "Planet Rock?" *(see Figure 8.8)*
It was the first rap song to use a drum machine instead of turntables.

15. By 1986, some hip-hop became mainstream. What was unique about Run-D.M.C.'s collaboration with Aerosmith in 1986? *(see Figure 8.9)*
It was a mix of rock and rap.

16. By 1986, hip-hop began to change. One group, Public Enemy (featuring Flavor Flav), wrote what kind of music? *(see Figure 8.10)*
Music about politics and social problems—"smart" or intellectual hip-hop

17. By 1987–1988, artists such as NWA, Ice-T, and Geto Boys rapped about tough life on the streets, gangs, crime, and poverty. What kind of music did they invent?
Gangsta rap

18. What is the art of imitating the sound of drums and scratching with the voice?
Beatboxing

19. What is the competitive art of using spray paint to tag buildings, subways, and other urban areas called?
Graffiti

20. Many rap songs, such as Vanilla Ice's "Ice Ice Baby" and Jay-Z's "Hard Knock Life," have traditionally used familiar songs to back up their music. What is this called? *(see Figure 8.11)*
Sampling

21. What is a popular way to change the sound of vocals in hip-hop today? (T-Pain is known for popularizing it.) *(see Figure 8.12)*
Using Auto-Tune

22. Today, rap has hybridized with other different styles of music—for example, country (Kid Rock) and swing/jazz (Outkast). Why is this important for hip-hop's future?
Hip-hop can appeal to listeners of all ages and backgrounds.

UNIT PROJECT

YOUR MISSION

In this project you will demonstrate your knowledge of a cultural element of hip-hop and use technology to illustrate what you have learned.

1. Choose one element of hip-hop that most interests you.

- DJing (also beatboxing, which imitates the DJ)
- Rap (MCing)
- Graffiti (the art of hip-hop)
- Dance (breakdancing/B-boying)
- Language (slang)
- Fashion

2. Research the topic to learn at least *ten* things you never knew about it, which you will in turn teach to the class. Use the Music Research Template (on next page). It will help you to research and list your basic facts.

3. Working alone or with a partner, create a project you can present to the class that demonstrates what you've learned.

4. Incorporate technology into the presentation—websites, blogs, PowerPoint, sequencers.

5. Present the project to the class.

Examples of projects include the following:

- Write a one-page bio of your favorite rapper or DJ and show slides.

- Use an online graffiti generator to share facts about graffiti's history—and show the class how you did it.

- Research old-school hip-hop fashion, and rap about some facts over a beat you find online.

- Demonstrate some websites that are important to the hip-hop underground and tell the class why.

- Design a webpage dedicated to the art of beatboxing.

Grading

25 points	Incorporate technology in some way.
25 points	Teach ten things about the subject to the class (2.5 points per item).
25 points	Present to the class.
25 points	Demonstrate creativity, effort, and teamwork (if applicable)—please see the following rubric.

100 points	*Totally awesome!*

Effort/Creativity/Focus Grading Rubric

0–5 points	I did almost nothing and put forth extremely low effort.
6–10 points	I did a little more than the minimum and put forth just a little effort.
11–15 points	I worked with average creativity and put forth average effort.
16–20 points	I did great work, had great focus, and put forth great effort.
21–25 points	I did top-notch work, showed superior creativity, and put forth excellent effort.

Music Research Notes

Fact 1	
Fact 2	
Fact 3	
Fact 4	
Fact 5	
Fact 6	
Fact 7	
Fact 8	
Fact 9	
Fact 10	

Figure 9.1

UNIT 9
The Music Biz

UNIT READING

The music business, sometimes known as the music biz, has changed quite a bit since the advent of the Internet. To understand how it operates now, it's important to consider the history of the business and how it has operated for about 150 years, since the first recordings were made in the late 1800s. This might be best told through a story about a fictional rock band called the Humongous Monsters.

The Life of a Rock Band

The year is 2003. The Humongous Monsters are an awesome rock band. They have become very popular in Ohio by playing shows in the biggest cities within a two-hour radius—Canton, Akron, Cleveland, and Columbus. Their demo CD has been circulating among music fans "in the know,"

and word is spreading about them through their MySpace account (hey, it's 2003). One evening after a show, a very cool-looking dude approaches the Humongous Monsters and tells them he is an A&R (artists and repertoire) scout from Raw Meat Records.

Record Labels

Raw Meat is a *record label*—a company that produces and sells music. The A&R scout looks and dresses like a typical fan, but he has a more serious agenda: he is seeking talent for the label and has the power to offer the band incentives to begin contract negotiations. The scout wouldn't come to the show unless the Humongous Monsters had already proven their ability to be successful on their own. The record label is interested in procuring talent that has already done a good deal of work getting themselves popular; they essentially want to purchase a business that is already up, running, functional, and profitable.

Advances

Once the Humongous Monsters enter negotiations with Raw Meat Records, there might be enticing talk about an *advance.* An advance is money given to an artist as an incentive upon signing. It is technically a large loan, because the company will withhold all sales, royalties, and profits from the artist until the advance amount is *recouped* (or earned back). It is the company's gamble that the musician will do well. Often, artists don't take into serious consideration that this money should be considered a means of living, rather than fun money to spend on clothes, cars, and jewelry. In this hypothetical case, the Humongous Monsters have received a pretty generous $125,000 advance.

Contracts

Before the Humongous Monsters decide to actually sign the contract, they should seek the advice of a music or entertainment lawyer. Often, contracts are dozens of pages long and are filled with complex legalese. The company hires a lawyer to write the contract with the specific purpose of maximizing profits and protecting the company's business interests. Musicians often don't understand how important it is to hire their own lawyer to strive for the same objective, with the artist's profits and career as the focus.

Royalties

Royalties are often discussed before contracts are signed. Royalties are what artists get whenever their music is played or sold. The funds can come from album sales, movie soundtracks, radio plays, commercials, and ringtone sales. Royalty rates are usually very slim for the artist and extremely profitable for the record label. The Humongous Monsters will get 10 to 20 percent of each physical copy album sale. For instance, if a song sells on iTunes for 99 cents, the record company will keep 61 cents, iTunes (Apple) will keep 29 cents, and the Humongous Monsters will take 9 cents.

Managers

The Humongous Monsters don't already have a band *manager,* so they are assigned one by Raw Meat Records. Managers have multiple duties, though their primary objective is to take care of all business aspects of the artist's career. They assist with the design of promotional materials, secure gigs, manage merchandising, collect and manage the cashflow, and make a business plan for the artist's career trajectory. In return, managers often collect approximately 15 to 20 percent of the artist's income. Choosing the right manager can make or break the band, but the reverse is also true—choosing the right band can make or break a manager!

Album Recording

Soon the Humongous Monsters will hit the studio to record their first professional album. During this process, they will consult with a *producer.* A producer's job is pretty similar to that of an athletic coach. The producer's goal is to help artists be the best they can. Producers are in charge of the recording process, selecting songs for the album, and giving singers and instrumentalists tips on playing better both individually and collectively. The producer can also be considered a creative director. The producer often determines whether the album is a success or failure.

Also hanging out in the studio is an *engineer.* He is the producer's helper and takes care of more technical aspects, such as setting up mics, running cables, and operating the mixer. Often young studio workers gain experience as engineers and later become producers.

Marketing

When the album is recorded, Raw Meat Records has made an investment in the artist and now needs to market the Humongous Monsters and get their music out there through targeted marketing. They will use many delivery systems to accomplish this goal: posters, apparel, videos, website ads, radio plays, television appearances, and more.

After all this, the music is finally released and hopefully people love it. Soon 100,000 albums will be sold, but the Humongous Monsters haven't earned a single dime on the sales yet. How could this be? Well, they're earning only about $1 for each $10 album sold, and they're still earning back their advance—so they haven't yet recouped the $125,000!

Touring

Okay, people from out of state have now heard the Humongous Monsters' hit song "You Can't Scare a Monster" on the radio, they have seen the video, and now they want to see the Humongous Monsters perform live in their town. It's time for the *concert promoter* to get to work. The promoter will arrange for the band's performance in a concert, handle contracts and negotiations, and sometimes even select other bands that will perform on a bill. Newer artists are often paired with experienced artists for tours, as they already have a guaranteed audience.

The promoter will also send *riders* to venues in advance of the performance. A rider is a set of instructions that must be followed by the venue before the concert takes place. Usually it details stage setup and lighting or sound-system requirements. However, sometimes these requests can be pretty outlandish. The artist best-known for starting the trend of ridiculous requests was the rock band Van Halen. On one tour, they made a request for a bowl of M&Ms to be placed backstage at each

of their shows, but all of the brown M&Ms were to be removed by hand. Although this sounds ludicrous, that same rider also detailed a certain proper stage setup necessary for the safety of the performers and the audience during the show. The band knew that if they found brown M&Ms backstage, then the venue management perhaps had not read the rider properly—causing potentially dangerous conditions onstage if they went through with the show. So there was actually a method behind the band's madness!

Roadies are also helpful during concerts and on tour. They travel with the band and are in charge of setting up and taking down musical equipment and stage sets, as well as sometimes tuning and repairing the instruments. They also might drive the band's van and mind the merchandise booth during the shows. Being a roadie is an excellent career option for someone who loves music but doesn't consider themselves to be musically inclined.

Promotion and Awards

Labels are relentless in their goal of selling music through the processes of market saturation and repetitive play. Raw Meat Records places Humongous Monsters songs in ads, movies, and on TV, hoping the repeated public exposure of the band takes hold, encouraging consumers to buy into the artist's musical offerings. If the Humongous Monsters are top sellers, they may be awarded Grammys, MTV awards, and gold or even platinum record sales awards.

Talent vs. Marketing

This is the point where talent and marketing become confusing. An artist need not be talented to sell well, and on the flip side, many talented musicians do not sell very well. However (in my opinion), an artist's total sales ultimately define whether he or she becomes known as legendary and influential. An average-skilled guitarist for a financially successful band can become an icon, have a guitar endorsement, and be hailed as a "rock god." Meanwhile, dozens of other guitarists with higher virtuostic abilities entertain in tiny bars, don't make enough money playing music to survive, and never get proper recognition. This is the music *business* after all, and often in business, profit trumps artistic merit.

Life After the Band Ends

After five albums and eight tours, the Humongous Monsters break up. They never became a huge hit band, but "You Can't Scare a Monster" made it into a movie, became a popular ringtone for about three months, and was even included in the video game *Guitar Master*. Ten years later, the band members continue to get monthly checks from *performing rights organizations* (PROs). PROs collect royalties from many sources that use the songs—radio, television, movies, ringtone companies, live clubs using the music, and so on—and send the money to artists on a regular basis. A single hit can provide a small source of steady income to an artist for years to come. The amount a songwriter receives for a single radio play is mere pennies, but if a couple hundred stations in the U.S. each play the song twice a day, those pennies can add up to hundreds or thousands of dollars per month for that artist. And that's just in one country—the U.S.!

Music 3.0

In 2013, the Humongous Monsters try to revive their career. However, the music biz has changed. Music producer/engineer Bobby Owsinski has defined our current musical era as "Music 3.0." The entire landscape of the music business is different from the way it's been for the last century. What's so different

about how artists need to work now than in the past? Record labels have lost total control over distribution sources, and the Internet has allowed musicians to communicate, market, and sell directly to fans. In the past, TV appearances and radio plays could amplify an artist's exposure and translate into album-sales figures. However, the Internet has allowed music pirates to flourish—today's most voracious music consumers (teens and young adults) no longer pay for their music. Even fans who don't spend time illegally downloading music can simply listen to their music for free on YouTube. Without recording sales to rely on, the Internet age has really impacted the way the business works.

Building a Tribe

Today, artists need a strong *tribe*. A "tribe" is a group of true fans. The artist's job is to lead the tribe, help it grow, communicate with its members, and provide them ways to invest in the artist without having to pay for music. An artist's primary income in Music 3.0 comes from merchandising and ticket sales at concerts.

Crowdfunding

There are many ways to sell product. Some artists have been experimenting with a couple of newer techniques, including *crowdfunding* and variable price points. Crowdfunding websites (such as Kickstarter) allow an artist to conceptualize a project (such as recording an album or going on tour) and ask fans to donate money to make it happen. Amanda Palmer, former pianist for the band the Dresden Dolls, leveraged her huge fanbase to collect more than $1 million in a Kickstarter campaign to pay for the recording of a solo album.

Variable Pricing

Variable price points allow an artist to get crowdfunding but are also used in other ways.

For example, for $5 an artist will offer fans a digital download of music. For $10, the artist might offer the digital download and a physical copy of the album. For $25, the artist might offer the download, the physical album, and a signed photo. For $250, the artist might offer the fan all of the above as well as a five-minute telephone conversation. Some artists, such as rock bands Radiohead and Nine Inch Nails, have allowed fans to pay whatever they want to download an album. Fans enjoy the flexibility of variable price points, and artists profit greatly from them.

Social Media

To stay connected and to keep the tribe interested, a good rule of thumb for an artist is to use social-network websites like Twitter and Facebook every day, blog every week, e-mail every month, and release music every six weeks or so. A constant stream of updates and releases really keeps the attention of the tribe. A savvy artist should also pay attention to social media metrics and statistics, and should be involved with multiple online music communities, such as Bandcamp, Last.fm, Sonicbids, SoundCloud, and Turntable.fm. Fans enjoy hearing from the artists and being able to communicate with them. Likewise, artists love knowing what their fans think and enjoy getting feedback from them. Music 3.0 is truly a collaborative artistic effort!

The Humongous Monsters have learned that the music biz is changing, and if you want to start making a living at it, you have an advantage over them. You now understand the history of the biz, but more importantly have access to the most powerful tool of Music 3.0—the Internet!

Figure 9.2 Advance

Figure 9.3 Signing a contract

STUDENT WORKSHEET

1. The A&R scout works for Raw Meat Records. What is a record label and what does it do?

2. The first person the Humongous Monsters encounter is the A&R scout. What does the scout do and how did he / she become interested in them?

3. Once the Humongous Monsters enter negotiations with Raw Meat Records, there might be enticing talk about an advance. What exactly is that? *(see Figure 9.2)*

4. Who should the Humongous Monsters consult with before signing a contract and why? *(see Figure 9.3)*

5. Royalties are often discussed before contracts are signed. What are royalties? Where do they come from?

6. With regard to royalties, how much do the Humongous Monsters (or other musicians) typically get per album? How much does Raw Meat Records get? What are the iTunes rates?

7. The Humongous Monsters don't already have a band manager, so they are assigned one by Raw Meat Records. Name at least three aspects of a manager's job. *(see Figure 9.4)*

Figure 9.4 A manager

8. Once the Humongous Monsters hit the studio to record their first professional album, they will consult with a producer. What does a producer do?

9. Also hanging out in the studio is an engineer. What is the engineer's job? *(see Figure 9.5)*

10. After the album is recorded, how does Raw Meat Records get the music out there (marketing)? Name three ways.

11. People love the music! A hundred thousand CDs were sold, but the Humongous Monsters haven't earned a dime yet. Why? *(see Figure 9.6)*

Figure 9.5 Recording the music

12. People from out of state have heard the Humongous Monsters' hit song "You Can't Scare a Monster" on the radio, they have seen the video, and now they want to see the Humongous Monsters perform live in their town. Who does the band need to call to help them and why?

13. Nobody is paying for music these days, so how does an artist make a living now?

Figure 9.6 Money flying out the door

14. What do the Humongous Monsters roadies do? *(see Figure 9.7)*

Figure 9.7 Tour bus

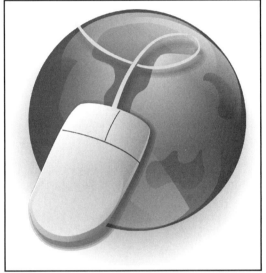

Figure 9.8 Internet power!

Figure 9.9 Your tribe

Figure 9.10 Social media for musicians

15. While on tour, the Humongous Monsters have a rider for their shows. What is a rider?

16. After five albums and eight tours, the Humongous Monsters break up. Ten years later, the members get monthly checks in the mail from performing rights organizations (PROs). What is a PRO and why do they send money to the Humongous Monsters?

17. The Humongous Monsters are trying to revive their career in 2013. However, the music biz has changed. Bobby Owsinski has defined our current musical era as "Music 3.0." What's so different about how artists need to work now than in the past? *(see Figure 9.8)*

18. What's a "tribe," and what should the Humongous Monsters do with it? *(see Figure 9.9)*

19. How often should artists stay in contact with their tribe?

20. What advantages do you have over the Humongous Monsters if you want to start making a living in the music biz? *(see Figure 9.10)*

Figure 9.2 Advance

Figure 9.3 Signing a contract

ANSWERS/STUDY GUIDE

1. The A&R scout works for Raw Meat Records. What is a record label and what does it do?

   A company that produces and sells music

2. The first person the Humongous Monsters encounter is the A&R scout. What does the scout do and how did he/she become interested in them?

   He seeks talent for the label—and looks for artists that have been very successful on their own.

3. Once the Humongous Monsters enter negotiations with Raw Meat Records, there might be enticing talk about an advance. What exactly is that? *(see Figure 9.2)*

   A large loan given to an artist when a contract is signed

4. Who should the Humongous Monsters consult with before signing a contract and why? *(see Figure 9.3)*

   An entertainment/music lawyer, because there is a lot of legal language involved and contracts are very long

5. Royalties are often discussed before contracts are signed. What are royalties? Where do they come from?

   Money artists get when their music is played or sold. Royalties come from album sales, radio plays, movie soundtracks, and ringtones.

6. With regard to royalties, how much do the Humongous Monsters (or other musicians) typically get per album? How much does Raw Meat Records get? What are the iTunes rates?

   The artist gets 10 to 20 percent per album, and the record label gets 80 to 90 percent. iTunes takes 29 cents per 99-cent download, the label takes 61 cents, and the artist takes 9 cents.

7. The Humongous Monsters don't already have a band manager, so they are assigned one by Raw Meat Records. Name at least three aspects of a manager's job. *(see Figure 9.4)*

   The manager takes care of all business aspects for the artist, gets gigs, creates a press/promo kit, collects and manages money, and makes a business plan.

8. Once the Humongous Monsters hit the studio to record their first professional album, they will consult with a producer.

Figure 9.4 A manager

What does a producer do?

Coaches the artist to be better, selects songs for an album, drives the studio, and makes the beats in rap music

9. Also hanging out in the studio is an engineer. What is the engineer's job? *(see Figure 9.5)*

   He is the producer's helper, who takes care of all the technical aspects, such as mics, wires, the mixer, the computer, and so on.

10. After the album is recorded, how does Raw Meat Records get the music out there (marketing)? Name three ways.

    CD sales, posters, T-shirts, videos, website/Internet, radio plays

11. People love the music! A hundred thousand CDs were sold, but the Humongous Monsters haven't earned a dime yet. Why? *(see Figure 9.6)*

    They haven't paid back their advance yet!

12. People from out of state have heard their hit song "You Can't Scare a Monster" on the radio, they have seen the video, and now they want to see the Humongous Monsters perform live in their town. What exactly does a booking agent do?

    Arranges for a band's performance in concert, handles paperwork and negotiations, selects other bands on the bill

13. Nobody is paying for music these days, so how does an artist make a living now?

    Tours, merchandise sales, other kinds of royalties. CD/iTunes sales are only about 10 percent of total income—max!

14. What do the Humongous Monsters roadies do? *(see Figure 9.7)*

    Set up and take down all stage and musical equipment, sometimes drive the van, sometimes run a T-shirt/CD table at the show

15. While on tour, the Humongous Monsters have a rider for their shows. What is a rider?

    A list of things an artist needs at a venue for them to perform

16. After five albums and eight tours, the Humongous Monsters break up. Ten years later, the members get monthly checks from performing rights organizations (PROs). What is a PRO and why do they send money to the Humongous Monsters?

    PROs collect and mail out royalties from radio plays, CD sales, and so on.

Figure 9.5 Recording the music

Figure 9.6 Money flying out the door

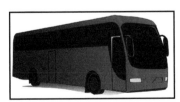

Figure 9.7 Tour bus

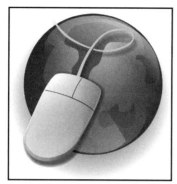

Figure 9.8 Internet power!

Figure 9.9 Your tribe

Figure 9.10 Social media
for musicians

17. The Humongous Monsters are trying to revive their career in 2013. However, the music biz has changed. Bobby Owsinski has defined our current musical era as "Music 3.0." What's so different about how artists need to work now than in the past? *(see Figure 9.8)*

    Artists communicate, market, and sell directly to fans.
    Labels, TV, and radio are irrelevant.
    Singles are more popular than albums.

18. What's a "tribe," and what should the Humongous Monsters do with it? *(see Figure 9.9)*

    An artist's true fans are a tribe. The Humongous Monsters need to lead, grow, communicate with, market to the tribe (with respect and with special things!).

19. How often should artists stay in contact with their tribe?

    They should tweet every day; blog every week; email every month; release music every six weeks; use YouTube, Facebook, Bandcamp, and Last.fm; and pay attention to social media metrics and statistics.

20. What advantages do you have over the Humongous Monsters if you want to start making a living in the music biz? *(see Figure 9.10)*

    You have the Internet, and you have the knowledge from this book.

UNIT PROJECT

YOUR MISSION

You are starting an independent record label. What kind of business do you want to set up for yourself? Answer thoughtfully and thoroughly on a separate piece of paper.

1. What will your label's name be? Invent a clever name to be remembered by your audience. (5)

2. What will your label's motto be? This should be short and catchy, like "I'm Lovin' It" (McDonald's) or "Live Mas" (Taco Bell). (5)

3. What will your label's mission be? This should be longer than your motto and should state exactly what you want to accomplish as a label. "Our mission is to…" This will state *why* you are selling music! (5)

4. What genre (type) of music will you specialize in? Why? Be specific. (5)

5. Design a logo for your label. It should be simple, effective, and memorable. Draw it. (5)

6. You need to sign an artist that will represent your label, your ideas, and your business. Check out www.unsigned.com. Browse by genre and choose *one* artist that will kick-start your label's success. Provide a brief description of the band and its style. (5)

7. You have $1,000 to pilot your label. It will cost $1,000 to print 500 copies of your band's first album (a cost of $2 per album). A thousand dollars is all you have to work with, so be creative!

   - How much will you charge for the CD? (5)
   - How much will you charge if you put the music on a flash drive, a record album, or a cassette and sell it? (5)
   - How much will you advance to the band? (5)
   - How much will you pay yourself? (5)

8. How will you sell the recording:

   - Who will you be selling the record to (and who wants to buy this kind of music)? (5)
   - How will you convince these people that your record is worth the purchase? (5)
   - You won't be able to put it on shelves at Target or Walmart—you only have $1,000! So where will you sell it? (5)
   - How will you spread the word? (5)

9. How will you promote your band /artist:

   - How will you market your album in different cities /clubs /states /countries? (5)
   - What kinds of websites will you use for promotion? (5)
   - What special items /promotions will you design for your most hardcore fans? (5)
   - What kinds of contests or giveaways will you hold? (5)

10. Set two simple five-year business goals. Make them realistic—not "We want to be millionaires with mansions," because that's not going to happen!

    - Goal 1 (2.5)
    - Goal 2 (2.5)
    - What would you like to see your record label actively doing five years from now? (5)

Grading

Each question has the number of points indicated in parentheses.

100 points ....*Totally awesome!*

Figure 10.1

UNIT 10
DJ HISTORY AND CULTURE

UNIT READING

Disc jockeys, or DJs, have been playing other people's music for years. However, DJing can be an extremely creative profession, especially with regard to how that music is presented. Genres vary, technology varies (DJs might use turntables, iPods, or digital controllers), venues vary (it might be in a loft, a club, or outdoors), and crowds vary (mixed ages at a wedding, people wanting to dance, or people needing background music while they dine or mingle). There are also many types of DJs—radio DJs, club DJs, mobile DJs, scratch DJs, and more. Regardless of these variables, it is a DJ's job to read the crowd, choose great music, put that music into a context the audience will understand, and deliver it with professionalism and flair. Let's take a closer look at DJing, some of its most important innovators, and its changing nature.

EQUIPMENT

Analog Mixers

First, let's discuss some of the equipment a DJ uses. A central piece of gear to a DJ is the *mixer*. A traditional analog mixer can control the outputs of two turntables (Technics SL-1200 MK2 is the most popular model) or CD players. Its capabilities allow a DJ to fade songs in and out, adjust volumes and equalization of tracks, add sound effects, and crossfade between two songs (simultaneously fading one song out to silence while fading another in to full volume).

Digital Mixers

Digital mixers, when used cooperatively with DJ software on a computer to play sound files, can be even more powerful. They can sample one-shot snippets of a song as it plays, which the DJ can then use to add variety to the soundscape. Digital mixers can loop sections of a tune, allowing other musical and vocal elements to be laid on top. "Hot cues" allow playback to be started from any point in a song. Songs can also be transposed to different keys, played in reverse, sped up or slowed down, "scratched," cued in a playlist, and played simultaneously in perfect rhythmic alignment with another song in a "mashup."

Digital Hardware and Software

A DJ *digital controller* is a piece of hardware that can be plugged into a computer to manipulate music. The hardware is linked to DJing software, which serves as the brain of the operation. Some examples of software include Serato Scratch Live, Mixxx, TRAKTOR, and VirtualDJ (both of which have a great free version). TRAKTOR features four playback decks, assignable hot cues, and effects processing. Serato is an interesting hybrid that allows tactile control of digital music and effects. Serato uses "dummy" time code vinyl records or CDs to give the DJ a physical feel of mixing. These time-coded platters don't actually contain audio information, but rather trigger MP3s to play. Interestingly, Serato also allows for mixing and remixing of video.

EVOLUTION OF THE DJ

DJing as a profession officially began on the radio in the early 1900s. Most music on the radio at that time was performed live, and radio stations even had live bands on the payroll. The DJ's job was primarily to be an announcer. In the 1930s, radio disc jockey Martin Block came out with a show called *Make Believe Ballroom.* On the show, he played recorded music but pretended to be broadcasting live from a party.

Club DJs

Nightclubs have been around since the early 1900s (in the form of honkytonks or speakeasy bars), and recorded music was played at these dance clubs, but only on jukeboxes—not by a live DJ. In 1947, French singer Régine Zylberberg created a nightclub in Paris called the Whisky à Go-Go; it was special because the jukebox was replaced by two turntables and a live DJ, and it was enhanced with colored lights and a dance floor. This was the beginning of the *discothèque.*

In 1950s America, radio DJs began to play music at *sock hops* (a dance party)—and DJ Bob Casey brought the two-turntables concept to America. Also at this time, Jamaica sprung alive with "sound system" culture, with DJs throwing large dance parties that featured ridiculously huge sound systems.

DJ Pioneer Francis Grasso

Francis Grasso is arguably one of the most important DJs of all time. He pioneered beatmatching in the late 1960s. He used headphones to allow him to preview the song about to be played, so that he could adjust its tempo to match the speed of the song already playing using the pitch control of the turntable (in other words, beatmatching or syncing beats per minute [BPM]). This allowed the music to continue from one song to the next uninterrupted, so that dancers didn't have to stop dancing. What was most important about Grasso was that he didn't play just any music for the crowd—he consciously selected music based upon the audience's energy, responding to their vibe and even controlling crowd dynamics.

Grandmaster Flash and Turntablism

Grandmaster Flash was also an influential and highly creative DJ. Influenced by Jamaican Kool Herc's massive block parties in the South Bronx of New York City, Flash also threw parties and was one of the founding DJs of hip-hop. Flash's great innovation was the pioneering use of backspinning and beatmatching records live. Taking a "cue" from the great DJ Kool Herc, he was also known for perfecting the extension of the disco break. He would take two copies of the same record and isolate what he considered to be the best few seconds of a song (usually the instrumental or drumming break). Juggling back and forth between two turntables, he would play that break repeatedly, laying down a rhythmic bed for breakdancers (or B-boys) to dance to and MCs to rap over. Using this technique while also perfecting the scratch (an innovation of Grand Wizzard Theodore), Grandmaster Flash began to turn the turntables into as much an actual instrument as a technology to play songs. This became known as *turntablism*.

Radio DJs

Radio DJs initially had the freedom to play whatever songs they wanted. Listeners could call in their favorites, and DJs could really express their personality through the songs they played. Today, only some college radio DJs have this creative freedom—most mainstream radio shows are preprogrammed by the minute and are even distributed generically across the country.

Live DJs

Live DJs, however, have always had the freedom to play whatever songs they wanted. Artists like The Electifying Mojo (Detroit) and Afrika Bambaataa (NYC) weren't so much known for their technical and musical manipulations of records, but rather for their ability to curate musical selections. Their choices were never narrow, and one might hear unusual B-side tracks or strange juxtapositions of different tunes. They might follow The Temptations with AC/DC, leading into a P-Funk song with a television theme or commercial jingle thrown in. Their art was that of the unexpected, making surprising

connections between amazing songs from all genres.

TECHNOLOGICAL ADVANCES

Technology has shaped the way DJs operate in positive and negative ways. With the advent of the MP3 and laptop computers, DJs are no longer limited to the crates of records they happen to bring to a club. Now their collection can span thousands of songs, and part of the art of DJing now is whittling down what to play. At one time, obscure tracks printed on limited-edition vinyl were only available to a handful of savvy DJs who could then use them to unexpectedly tear up the dance floor. Now, these rarities can be accessible to everyone. This then attenuates the risks a DJ is willing to take when choosing music, as often only proven tracks are played. Likewise, DJ sets on the whole have become more predictable because the same proven music is often selected night after night, regardless of which DJ is entertaining.

New Era of DJing

On the other hand, many new, positive ways to manipulate pre-recorded music have become available through the use of technology. Loop controls enable DJs to grab any section of a song on the fly, sample it, repeat it, assign the sample to a "hot cue" button, and play that sample at any time. DJs can layer multiple samples, and a song can easily be distorted beyond recognition with onboard effects processing.

Technology's diminishing cost has also made DJing more popular—more people can afford the equipment. It has therefore become easier for almost anybody with a passion for music to secure a "DJ night" at a club, as a means to play their favorite songs for their group of friends. Some DJs feel this has cheapened the profession a bit, because the newer jockeys don't have as much interest in becoming better DJs, learning new techniques for mixing, or really trying to find good music. The most difficult, but most artistic and rewarding, aspect of DJing has always been song selection—especially to respond to, react to, or challenge a crowd. Playing the right song at the right time or moving through the right sequence of songs can build excitement and energy in a dancing crowd. Or, it can otherwise rekindle an audience's participation if their fervor begins to dwindle.

EDM

Many of today's hottest DJs are actually *EDM* (electronic dance music) artists that create their own music geared toward large dance parties or raves. Often, they essentially DJ their own music (a pre-recorded backing track), over which they improvise and ad-lib parts to give it a live feel. Recent DJs like Kaskade, Tiesto, Skrillex, and David Guetta have risen to superstar status and earn millions per year as entertainers.

DJing as a Career

DJing as a career path can offer a variety of opportunities. Traditionally, DJs can work at radio stations, wedding receptions, social events, and parties. People can also DJ as instrumentalists, providing tracks for rappers or bands. Music supervisors create soundtracks for stores or brands, such as The Gap or Starbucks. These soundtracks are important because they reinforce the aesthetic and design of the store. Those who are more interested in the technical end of things can work as electrical engineers, designers, and programmers of new DJ hardware and software that take the field in new directions.

DJs can be thought of as musicians. DJs *do* need to think in musical terms—such as blending rhythms or key signatures of two songs, or understanding the architecture of a song to know where a break or bridge happens. They are also entertainers, keeping the crowd engaged and dancing.

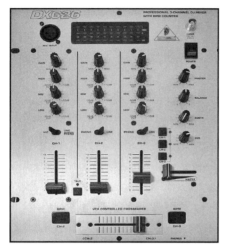

Figure 10.2 Behringer DX626 mixer

Figure 10.3 Technics SL-1200 MK2

Figure 10.4 Young woman plays a gramophone, air raid shelter, North London (1940)

Figure 10.5 Régine Zylberberg

STUDENT WORKSHEET

1. What is a mixer's job? *(see Figure 10.2)*

2. What does the crossfader do?

3. What is the number one DJ turntable? *(see Figure 10.3)*

4. From the 1900s to the 1940s, what function did DJs have in nightclubs and on the radio? *(see Figure 10.4)*

5. From the 1940s to the 1990s, DJs had great musical freedom. Since then, what's changed about the way DJs choose songs on the radio?

6. In 1947, Régine Zylberberg created a nightclub in Paris called a discothèque. This was copied in America with DJ Bob Casey's sock hops and in Jamaica's "sound system" culture. What did she do? *(see Figure 10.5)*

7. Why was Francis Grasso (1960s) one of the most important DJs of all time? *(see Figure 10.6)*

8. What contributions did Grandmaster Flash (1970s) bring to DJing? *(see Figure 10.7)*

Figure 10.6 DJ Greg Stainer

Figure 10.7 Grandmaster Flash

Figure 10.8 Records in their DJ crates

Figure 10.9 Mixxx for the digital DJ

9. What is turntablism? Name one of its techniques.

10. DJs used to carry crates of records around to their gigs. How has the invention of MP3s changed the way DJs do business? Name a positive and a negative consequence. *(see Figure 10.8)*

11. DJing has gone digital. What are some of the top DJ software titles? *(see Figure 910.9)*

12. What is time-code vinyl?

13. What is a hot cue?

14. What does it mean to sync BPMs? *(see Figure 10.10)*

15. What is pitch control on a turntable? *(see Figure 10.11)*

16. What is a loop control on digital DJ software?

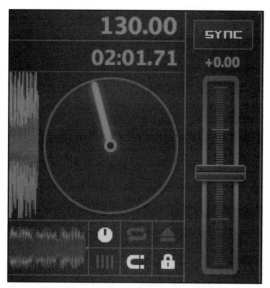

Figure 10.10 Closeup showing BPMs and Sync button

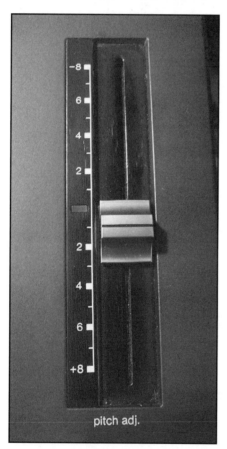

Figure 10.11 Turntable pitch control

Figure 10.12 EDM festival concert

17. What has all this technology done to cheapen the profession of DJing?

18. What is the most difficult, most artistic, most rewarding, and most challenging skill a DJ must learn to master?

19. What is EDM? Where is it featured? *(see Figure 10.12)*

20. The 2000s have ushered in an era of superstar DJs that earn millions per year. Name two.

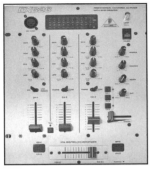

Figure 10.2 Behringer DX626 mixer

Figure 10.3 Technics SL-1200 MK2

Figure 10.4 Young woman plays a gramophone, air raid shelter, North London (1940)

Figure 10.5 Régine Zylberberg

Figure 10.6 DJ Greg Stainer

ANSWERS/STUDY GUIDE

1. What is a mixer's job?

   Mixers blend all the music, fade songs in/out, and adjust volumes and mics.

2. What does the crossfader do? *(see Figure 10.2)*

   It fades one song out while simultaneously fading another in.

3. What is the number-one DJ turntable? *(see Figure 10.3)*

   The Technics 1200 turntable—the most popular DJ turntable ever. It is built like a Mercedes.

4. From the 1900s to the 1940s, what function did DJs have in nightclubs and on the radio? *(see Figure 10.4)*

   Music was usually played live—not from a record—so DJs made announcements rather than playing tunes.

5. From the 1940s to the 1990s, DJs had great musical freedom. Since then, what's changed about the way DJs choose songs on the radio?

   DJs no longer have control over what is played; they don't choose their own music. Everything is preplanned out by the minute, and DJs are broadcast to multiple cities simultaneously.

6. In 1947, Régine Zylberberg created a nightclub in Paris called a discothèque. This was copied in America with DJ Bob Casey's sock hops and in Jamaica's "sound system" culture. What did she do? *(see Figure 10.5)*

   Instead of hiring live performers, she DJ'd with two turntables, a dance floor, and colored lights.

7. Why was Francis Grasso (1960s) one of the most important DJs of all time? *(see Figure 10.6)*

   He was the first to beatmatch and the first to use headphones to cue songs. He invented beatmatching, and he decided what songs to play based on how the crowd acted.

8. What contributions did Grandmaster Flash (1970s) bring to DJing? *(see Figure 10.7)*

   He extended the break sections of songs, he perfected the scratch, and he launched the art of turntablism.

9. What is turntablism? Name one of its techniques.

   The art of using turntables as musical instruments, with techniques such as cutting, beat juggling, scratching, needle drops, and back spinning.

10. DJs used to carry crates of records around to their gigs. How has the invention of MP3s changed the way DJs do business?

Figure 10.7 Grandmaster Flash

Figure 10.8 Records in their DJ crates

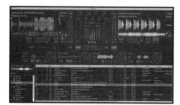

Figure 10.9 Mixxx—for the digital DJ

Figure 10.10 Closeup showing BPMs and Sync button

Figure 10.11 Turntable pitch control

Figure 10.12 EDM festival concert

Name a positive and a negative consequence.
(see Figure 10.8)
Positive: Now DJs have access to an unlimited number of songs.
Negative: Now everyone has the same music.

11. DJing has gone digital. What are some of the top DJ software titles? *(see Figure 10.9)*
Serato Scratch Live, TRAKTOR, Ableton Live, Mixxx, and VirtualDJ.

12. What is time-code vinyl?
It is a plastic platter that doesn't contain music but gives the DJ the feel of using actual records.

13. What is a hot cue?
It is a feature on digital mixers that lets a DJ start at any point in the song.

14. What does it mean to sync BPMs? *(see Figure 10.10)*
Sync means to "align." BPM means beats per minute. Syncing BPMs is when DJs match the speeds of two songs to keep the music going—beatmatching!

15. What is pitch control on a turntable? *(see Figure 10.11)*
It speeds up or slows down the music to allow BPM sync.

16. What is a loop control on digital DJ software?
Allows DJ to grab any section of a song on the fly, sample it, repeat it, and play that sample at any time.

17. What has all this technology done to cheapen the profession of DJing? *(see Figure 10.12)*
Anyone with basic equipment and a few friends can become a DJ at a club. Therefore, the quality of DJs is not as high.

18. What is the most difficult, most artistic, most rewarding, and most challenging skill a DJ must learn to master?
Choosing the right song at the right time, responding to the audience with a song selection that surprises, energizes, and so on

19. What is EDM? Where is it featured?
Electronic dance music. It is often featured at raves and house parties.

20. The 2000s have ushered in an era of superstar DJs that earn millions per year. Name two.
Kaskade, Skrillex, David Guetta, Tiësto, Swedish House Mafia, Steve Aoki, Deadmau5

UNIT PROJECT

Your Mission

Create a "mix tape" of 10 songs that flow well together, and demonstrate five basic DJing techniques using Mixxx or Virtual DJ software. Your teacher will provide you with a flash drive or folder of school-appropriate songs, or you may use your own MP3 collection with permission.

1. Insert your flash drive first. When you open Mixxx/Virtual DJ,, it will ask you where your Music Library is—please find your folder of MP3s.

2. Click on the Playlist tab from the column on the left side. Then choose Create a New Playlist.

3. Once the playlist is created, click back on the library and search for songs you'd like to include. You must choose 10 songs. Drag the songs onto your playlist's name to add them.

4. Make sure that all the songs you choose are clean versions, and are appropriate for school. You will be sharing your mixes out loud in class!

5. Choose carefully—create a set of songs that work well together, that are in similar styles or speeds, that tell a story, or that simply flow well from one song to the next.

6. Once you have selected all 10 of your songs, click back on your playlist and arrange them in the order you'd like them to be played. Write down the list of songs using the DJ Project Worksheet that accompanies this unit.

7. Plan ahead and write down on the Project Worksheet which DJ techniques you will use during which songs/transitions. Also write down the BPMs of your songs. Grouping songs with similar BPMs is a strong DJing technique.

8. Write down how the songs flow together, what makes them work as a set, what they have in common, and so on.

9. You need to include only 15 to 20 seconds of each song on your final "mixtape," after which you will fade out from one song and into the next. You must keep the mix going!

10. Practice mixing the flow of songs, along with the techniques.

11. When you have practiced the entire set, click on Recording and then Start Recording. You should then start your mix. When you're done, click Stop Recording and save it. That's what will be played for the class. Include your name as part of the title of the final file.

12. If you have the time and the right equipment, you may choose to even perform the DJ set live for the class.

The DJ Techniques (Choose 5)

1. **Crossfader:** Use the Crossfader between songs.

2. **Sync BPMs:** Use BPM (beats per minute) detection to identify two songs close to the same speed, and sync them for a few seconds as one fades out and another fades in. You may choose to use just an instrumental portion of one of the songs if it blends better.

3. **Pitch/Rate control:** Adjust the Pitch/Rate slider during any song—it is often effective at the end of a song to slow the speed—just before you move into the next song.

4. **Scratch:** Use the Scratch function during any song.

5. **Loop tools:** Use the Loop tools during any song. It is effective to start with a long loop and then continuously halve it with each consecutive repetition. Or, start with a short

one and continuously double it with each repetition. It can also be used to transition from one song to the next.

6. **Hot Cue:** This is a bit more challenging. Set up some hot cues in advance to allow you to jump to a predetermined section of the song.

Grading

10 points .... Create a handwritten playlist—ten songs.

10 points .... Create a handwritten list of both BPMs and 5 of the DJ techniques used during each song transition— preplan this!

10 points .... Identify how the songs flow together, what makes them work as a set, what they have in common, and so on.

10 points .... Finalized recording of the mix-tape set.

10 points .... The mixtape should have 10 song snippets, each 20 seconds or less.

25 points .... Use five of the six listed DJ techniques.

25 points .... Demonstrate effort, creativity, and focus. (See the following rubric.)

100 points .... *Totally awesome!*

Effort / Creativity / Focus Grading Rubric

0–5 points .... I did almost nothing and gave extremely low effort.

6–10 points .... I did a little more than the minimum and gave just a little effort.

11–15 points ...... I worked with average creativity and gave average effort.

16–20 points ...... I did great work, had great focus, and gave great effort.

21–25 points ...... I did top-notch work, showed superior creativity, and gave excellent effort.

UNIT PROJECT WORKSHEET

Please note the BPM for each song and each of the 5 DJ techniques you used. Please also note with a + or – sign if you have decided to change the BPM for any song.

Song Title	Artist	BPM / Technique
1. _____	_____	_____
2. _____	_____	_____
3. _____	_____	_____
4. _____	_____	_____
5. _____	_____	_____
6. _____	_____	_____
7. _____	_____	_____
8. _____	_____	_____
9. _____	_____	_____
10. _____	_____	_____

- How do the songs flow together?
- What makes them work as a cohesive set?
- What do the songs have in common?
- How did you use BPMs to guide your decision-making as a DJ?

Figure 11.1

UNIT 11
LISTENING TO LEARN AND LEARNING TO LISTEN

UNIT READING

In this unit, you will dive deeply into a song of your choice (provided it is school-appropriate) to become an expert on your favorite music. Once the tune is approved, you will be given a series of questions that require you to gather information about the song, its origins, and its content. Using the Internet, you must find answers to questions such as:

• What instruments were used in the song?

• What is the form of the song?

• Why was the song written?

• Is there a theme or message in the lyrics?

ASSIGNMENT

Create a PowerPoint or Prezi presentation that will enable you to dig into the meaning of the song's words. You'll present each stanza of the lyrics in a single slide and write, in your own words, what you believe the singer means by those lyrics. You are responsible for defining unknown words, pointing out figurative language, and breaking down double entendres. Incorporating pictures, colors, and transitions can help you make the presentation more appealing.

When your PowerPoint/Prezi is complete, play the song for the class and share what it's all about. This project should help you think more deeply about your favorite music than you ever have, and you'll build technology chops using PowerPoint or Prezi as a powerful presentation-delivery system. This can easily be a multiweek project.

You must answer all the following questions—if you don't know the answer, look it up! Check Wikipedia for basic facts, and use www.songfacts.com for info on popular songs.

GENERAL INFO

Do a little research and answer these questions. Point values are indicated after each question.

1. Your name

2. Artist's name

3. Song title

4. Album

5. Record label (5)

6. Year written/released (5)

7. Genre (be as specific as possible) (5)

8. Is the song typical of this genre? Why or why not? (5)

9. What other artists would you recommend to a person who likes listening to music written by your chosen artist? (Name two others.) (5)

10. What is an interesting fact about the artist? (5)

11. What is an interesting fact about the song? (5)

12. Identify all instruments used in the song. (5)

13. How was technology used to create the song? (5)

14. What is the form/structure of the song? For example: Verse 1–Chorus–Verse 2–Chorus–Bridge–Chorus (5)

15. Why was the song written? (If there is no definite answer, why do you think it was written?) (5)

THINKING ABOUT THE SONG

Answer in complete sentences. These facts likely will not be found online—formulate your own answers!

- What is the primary message the artist is trying to get across? (5)

- Who is the audience of the song? Does it appeal only to specific listeners? (5)

- What is the mood of the song? How does it make you feel? (5)

- What does the song seem to value? What is important to the artist? (5)

- Is there a political stance to the song? If so, what is it? (5)

- Is there a social message to the song? If so, what is it? (5)

- What does this song offer that others don't? What is unique about it? (5)

- Write another verse (at least eight lines) to the song that carry the same message or storyline the artist has already written. (10)

---

100 points ....*Totally awesome!*

Now move on to making that PowerPoint or Prezi. Identify all the imagery, symbolism, and figures of speech (metaphors, similes, and alliteration) in the lyrics. Also, look up any words or slang that you don't know. Become the expert on this song!

UNIT PROJECT

YOUR MISSION

You will create a PowerPoint or Prezi presentation outlining a detailed analysis of the song's lyrics. Finally, you will share your project with the class.

1. First make sure you have completed the questions before beginning your PowerPoint/Prezi.

2. Make sure you can summarize the song's meaning before starting and that you can explain the message that the verses and chorus are trying to get across.

3. Copy the song's lyrics into a PowerPoint /Prezi presentation. You'll find the lyrics

online. Use a two-content layout if you're using PowerPoint.

- Lyrics should be copied to the *left* side of each slide.
- Your analysis should be written on the *right* side of each slide.
- Each line should be numbered for reference.
- Each section of the song (verse, chorus, bridge) should get its own slide.
- Duplicate the slides as necessary and customize!
- Analyze the lyrics and type the meanings directly into the presentation.

4. Present the song for the class. When you present, make sure you:

- Give a one- to two-sentence synopsis of what the song is about.
- Start the PowerPoint/Prezi and let the other students read the lyrics as the song plays.
- When the song is finished, describe the primary message of the song.
- Walk the class through the lyric analysis.
- Include the class in discussing the lyrics. They may have alternate interpretations!

Remember to speak loudly, slowly, and clearly. Also maintain eye contact with your audience.

Grading

100 points ....Complete the Listening to Learn and Learning to Listen worksheet correctly.

100 points ....Complete the PowerPoint/Prezi correctly.

100 points ....Give the presentation correctly.

300 points ....*Totally awesome!*

LISTENING TO LEARN AND LEARNING TO LISTEN CLASS WORKSHEET

Your Mission

You will do some thoughtful writing about each of the songs your classmates present.

Your listening/writing exercises are to be written in complete sentences, in paragraph form. You should always read your writing back to yourself to check for errors, to ensure your writing fits the assignment, and that it is clear and easy to read! Make sure you:

- Use of a clear topic sentence and a strong conclusion.
- Explain ideas with sufficient/relevant details.
- Use content-specific vocabulary.
- Vary sentence beginnings/lengths.
- Use end marks and commas correctly.

Paragraph 1: Descriptive

When you write, begin with a topic sentence and then use colorful adjectives to describe the music. Also, describe the music using at least four of the following descriptive characteristics music can possess:

- Instrumentation/Timbre
- Types of voices/number of voices
- Tempo/speed
- Rhythm
- Dynamics/volume level
- Emotional content/mood
- Lyrical meaning
- Form/structure (verse/chorus, ABA, variations, repetitions, and so on)
- Texture (complex, simple, busy, open, and so on)
- Production methods (if known)
- Cultural elements and influence

Example Paragraph

The song "Heartless" by Kanye West is a slow and gloomy dirge that addresses a romantic relationship the singer has with a woman that has begun to disintegrate and dissolve. The lyrics depict a close couple that has been torn apart and highlight the emotions of loneliness, bitterness, and frustration felt by the singer. Driven by a sampled guitar from a 1984 Alan Parsons tune and the simple sound of the TR-808 drum machine, the tune takes on a slight reggae feel. It is highlighted by minimal keyboards, special echo effects (during the bridge section), and Kanye's Auto-Tuned voice (at times even providing his own vocal harmonies).

Part 1 Grading

5 points ....Topic sentence

20 points ....Four descriptive characteristics (5 points each)

_____

25 points ....*Totally awesome!*

PARAGRAPH 1: PERSONAL

When you write, become a music critic. Describe what you like or dislike about various aspects of the music, and explain why you feel this way. Imagine why someone else with different tastes than you may or may not care for the song. Remain objective, even if it isn't the type of music you listen to. Someone reading your description and opinion should be able to tell that you are *open-minded* about music.

Example Paragraph

Kanye West has done a wonderful job of bringing an obscure sample to life and should be credited with creating such a heartfelt love song out of such simplicity. He delivers the message of the song with conviction.

"Heartless," a gentle R&B-style love song about heartbreak and loneliness, could be recommended to anyone going through a difficult time in a romantic relationship.

Part 2 Grading

15 points ....Three reasons supporting your opinion of the song (5 points for each reason)

5 points ....One reason why someone may have a different opinion from you do

5 points ....A conclusion sentence (could be a recommendation to a listener)

_____

25 points ....*Totally awesome!*

Figure 12.1

UNIT 12
FIELD TRIP SUPPLEMENT EXAMPLES

YOUR MISSION

Research jobs in the music industry, with special focus on the destinations you'll visit as a class. You will need to do most of this research on the Internet. Take time to learn about the places you'll be visiting—you will gain more from the experience and be better prepared to ask great questions of your hosts. Answer on a separate sheet of paper, please!

STUDENT WORKSHEET 1

CONCERT VENUES

Figure 12.2

Part 1

Worth 50 points—3 points each.

1. Name five performers who be appearing at the concert venue in the next few months.

2. What kind of clientele does the concert venue cater to?

3. What are some unique aspects of the concert venue?

4. Does the venue host events other than concerts? What kinds of events do they have?

5. What is backline equipment and what does the concert venue provide?

6. Tell a little about the history of the venue. Give three facts.

Concert Venue: Jobs and Careers

Briefly define the responsibilities of jobs available at the concert venue. Try doing a Google search for each, such as "talent buyer live concert job responsibility."

1. Talent buyer

2. Sound engineer

3. Manager

4. Director of sales

5. Door host

6. Marketing director

7. Club owner

8. Entertainers

9. Roadie

STUDENT WORKSHEET 2

LOCAL RECORDING STUDIO

Figure 12.3

1. Name at least five artists who have recorded at the studio.

2. What else is recorded here, apart from artists/musicians? For example, do they do commercials or voice-overs?

3. Provide a history of the studio. For example: How long has it been around? Who started it?

4. Give three facts about what's in the studio. Do they have any interesting equipment? Are there any special amenities for clients?

5. How much does it cost to rent the space and record at the studio?

6. What does it take to be an intern at the studio? Are there any jobs available? What are their requirements?

7. What are some interesting facts about the owners or engineers? (Give three.)

Recording Studio: Jobs and Careers

Define the responsibilities of jobs available at the studio. Try doing a Google search for each, such as "engineer recording studio job responsibility."

1. Office manager

2. Sound engineer

3. Producer

4. Intern

5. Studio Technician

6. Runner

7. Mastering Engineer

STUDENT WORKSHEET 3

Figure 12.4

Local Radio Station

1. Tell a little about the history of the radio station. Give three facts.

2. How far does the radio station signal reach?

3. What is a transmitter?

4. What is a Public Service Announcement?

5. What is the Emergency Broadcasting System?

6. What is a Station Identification?

7. Describe how FM broadcasting works.

8. What are some of the regular shows the radio station features? Name three.

Define the responsibilities for each radio station job. Try doing a Google search for each, such as "operations manager radio station job."

1. Operations Manager

2. Marketing/Promotions

3. Music Director

4. DJ

Use information from the Internet to describe how you could start your own radio station at school. Do not make up answers; research and write something that could potentially work. Make sure to include information on:

1. Equipment

2. Costs

3. The FCC/legal issues

4. Who would run it.

STUDENT WORKSHEET 4

Figure 12.5

Local Music Retail Store

1. Explore the gear for sale. Suppose you have $5,000 to spend on whatever you'd like. What would you buy?

2. Name one musical instrument or item you're not familiar with. What does it do?

3. Are there any events happening in the store? Perhaps artist clinics or special sales promotions?

4. Tell a little about the history of the store.

5. What's the most expensive guitar you can find?

6. Do they sell any used gear? Will they buy or trade any of the personal gear you bring into the store?

7. What is financing? What is layaway? Do they offer either of those services?

8. Does the store offer private lessons?

9. What are some of the different areas of the store (for example, the drum department)?

Music Retail Store: Jobs and Careers

Define the responsibilities for each music retail store job. Try doing a Google search for each, such as "talent buyer live concert job responsibility."

1. Retail sales associate

2. Store manager

3. Drum or Guitar tech

4. Marketing manager

5. Teacher/lessons

Figure 12.6

STUDENT WORKSHEET 5

COLLEGE LEVEL RECORDING ARTS / MEDIA ARTS PROGRAM

1. What are some types of classes you would take while enrolled in a recording arts program? Name three.

2. How long does the program last?

3. What kinds of careers can you get with this degree? Name three.

4. What would you need to to do to get into the program? Is there an audition process? Do you need a certain high school GPA, or perhaps particular scores on the ACT or SAT?

5. Tell a little about the history of the school. Give three facts.

6. What are the housing options for the school? Do they offer dorm, commuter, or online options?

7. What kinds of classroom facilities do they have for learning?

8. What is the tuition per year? How about for the whole program?

9. Do they offer any special scholarships or financial aid?

10. Do they have any kind of summer or evening classes for individuals who are not currently students?

Figure II.1

PART 2

CREATIVE EXPRESSIONS

Part 2 of *Music Tech 101* focuses on the creation, collaboration and communication involved in music made with technology. Intensive projects include songwriting with software (looping/sequencing/multitracking), film scoring, creating music videos, remixing, using live interactive music systems, participating in remote/online collaboration, and working on individualized goals. Skills acquired in class will develop your creative artistry and expression.

Goals for Part 2

- Study songwriting

- Write songs in different styles

- Make sound effects for a short movie

- Play music and jam digitally with others in the classroom

- Make a video about music

- Remix music with loop-based software

- Turn your computer into a musical instrument

Figure II.2

MONKEY BEATS SONG

YOUR MISSION

Create a song with the Monkey Machine.

Resource

www.rinki.net/pekka/monkey X

Drum Programming

Lengthen each section to be 32 beats.

Points	Page	Section
6	00	Intro
6	01	Verse1.A
6	02	Verse1.B
6	03	Chorus.A
6	04	Chorus.B
6	05	Verse2.A (copy and paste section 01)
6	06	Verse2.B (copy and paste section 02)
6	07	Chorus.A (copy and paste section 03)
6	08	Chorus.B (copy and paste section 04)
6	09	Outro

60 points total for the music

Are they each 32 beats long? If not, subtract 3 points for each one that is shorter.

Lyrics

20 points ....Write lyrics for the song— they can be any topic you'd like! Use an online rhyming dictionary if you need help.

20 points ....Share the lyrics and drum beat together. (Record using Mixcraft, GarageBand, Audacity, or other DAW or perform it live!)

40 points ....Total for the lyrics

100 points ....*Totally awesome!*

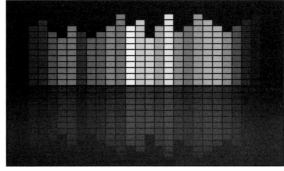

Figure II.3

POP SONGWRITING SESSION 1

YOUR MISSION

Create a song with Mixcraft, GarageBand, or Soundation using standard pop song format.

Resource

www.soundation.com ✓

You can use the website above for free, but it is recommended that you get a premium account which will give you access to thousands of loops.

Create a song in Mixcraft, GarageBand, or Soundation using the following pop song format:

Intro

Verse 1 (a)

Verse 1 (b)—builds the music a bit

Chorus (a)

Chorus (b)

Verse 2 (a)—similar to/same as Verse 1

Verse 2 (b)

Chorus (a)—similar to/same as the first chorus

Chorus (b)

Bridge—different music entirely

Chorus (a/b)

End/fade out

- Use at least eight different loops and blend at least two to three at a time on both

- Chorus and Verse
- Use the virtual instrument track at least once to create your own music
- Use effects to change your sounds on at least two tracks/instruments
- Manipulate at least one loop beyond recognition
- Important note for when you are finished: Make sure to share your finished song with others, and get their *positive* feedback on what you did well, and also *constructive* feedback on how you could take your songwriting skills to the next level!

Grading

10 points	Intro
10 points	Verse 1 (a), Verse 1 (b)—builds the music a bit
10 points	Chorus (a), Chorus (b)
10 points	Verse 2 (a)—similar/same as Verse 1, Verse 2 (b)
10 points	Chorus (a)—similar/same as other chorus, Chorus (b)
10 points	Bridge—different music entirely
10 points	Chorus (a/b), End/Fade Out
20 points	Virtual Instrument track at least once
20 points	Use at least 4 loops, 2–3 blended in the Verse
20 points	Use at least 4 different loops, 2-3 blended in the Chorus
20 points	Use the effects panel to change the sound on at least two instrument tracks
50 points	Effort, concentration, creativity, hard work using the rubric below

200 points	*Totally awesome!*

Effort/Creativity/Focus Grading Rubric

0–5 points	I did almost nothing and put forth extremely low effort.
6–10 points	I did a little more than the minimum and put forth just a little effort.
11–15 points	I worked with average creativity and put forth average effort.
16–20 points	I did great work, had great focus, and put forth great effort.
21–25 points	I did top-notch work, showed superior creativity, and put forth excellent effort.

POP SONGWRITING SESSION 2

YOUR MISSION

Create another song with Mixcraft, GarageBand, or Soundation using a standard pop-song structure. This time, your song must be:

- In a different style/genre. For example, if you wrote a hip-hop tune for your first song, you should try writing a rock or techno song for this session.
- In a different mood/emotion. For example, if you wrote an energetic or happy song, try writing a sad or aggressive song for this session.
- Follow the instructions for Pop Songwriting Session 1, but expand your musical wings.
- Some positive emotions to write about might include: happy, joyful, excited, elated, thrilled, energetic, enthusiastic, peppy, animated, calm, cheerful, relaxed, blissful,

- balanced, stable, secure, glad, sunny, merry, and so on.

- Some negative emotions to write about might include: angry, mad, sad, depressed, hateful, annoyed, irritated, livid, irate, furious, miserable, gloomy, down, unhappy, low, aggravated, bothered, upset, hopeless, and so on.

- Use the same grading rubric as Pop Songwriting Session 1.

- Don't forget to *share* your music, and get *positive* feedback as well as *constructive* feedback from others on how to take your songwriting skills to the next level!

- Important Note: Once you've completed two pop songs, move on to a different piece of software and write a couple more. This will build your flexibility and understanding of various digital audio workstations. Use any software you'd like or have available!

- Take Your Songwriting Even Further: You can manipulate the requirements in any way you'd like. For instance, perhaps one song will be written without loops and focus only on composing with virtual instruments. Or write a song that requires you to record a live vocal or instrumental track. Or pen a tune based on some samples you grabbed from another song or movie. Or collaborate with a partner in writing some music.

Figure II.4

POP SONGWRITING SESSION 3: REMIX!

YOUR MISSION

Create a remix of a classmate's Mixcraft, Audacity, GarageBand, or Soundation song.

Important: Make sure that once you open your partner's song, you immediately rename it to identify that it is a remix of the song. This will prevent you from accidentally overwriting the original. Don't destroy your partner's hard work!

Keep what's hot, manipulate or delete what's not!

Grading

20 points .... Manipulate at least existing four tracks/loops

15 points .... Add a new section (verse, chorus, and so on).

10 points .... Add a new intro and outro (5 points each).

15 points .... Add at least three new music loops.

5 points .... Add or change one drumbeat loop.

10 points .... Add effects to two different loops/instruments.

25 points .... Demonstrate effort, concentration, creativity, and focus. (Use rubric below)

---

100 points .... *Totally awesome!*

Effort/Creativity/Focus Grading Rubric

0–5 points .... I did almost nothing and put forth extremely low effort.

6–10 points .... I did a little more than the minimum and put forth just a little effort.

11–15 points ......I worked with average creativity and put forth average effort.

16–20 points ......I did great work, had great focus, and put forth great effort.

21–25 points ......I did top-notch work, showed superior creativity, and put forth excellent effort.

Figure II.5

MUSIC AND TECHNOLOGY MOVIEMAKING

YOUR MISSION

Create a short, entertaining movie about music and technology that will teach others something about a chosen topic.

The movie should:

- Teach something to the viewer—it is educational
- Be entertaining and creatively presented
- Be about music and technology in some way
- Be five minutes or less
- Include original music or sound effects
- Include a transition, title and credit sequences

The project should be structured in the following way. Some "levels" like Level 1 should only take one class period. Some may take several periods, like the editing that occurs during Level 7. This project may be done individually, but it's a lot more fun with a group.

Level 1: 50 Points

- Brainstorm topics (5 pts.) to decide on subject matter.
- Brainstorm how to present (5 pts.) the movie—talk show, sitcom, informational video, commercial, documentary, etc (list at least three ideas).
- Create a five minute framework (15 pts.) that gives guidelines on the structure and sequence minute by minute.
- Daily effort using rubric below (25 pts.)

Level 2: 50 Points

- Gather facts and do research (25 pts.)—you should have at least 10 to 20 specific and interesting facts relevant to your subject. Use the Music Research Template to organize and gather information.
- Create characters if you are not playing yourself in the movie
- Daily effort using rubric below (25 pts.)

Level 3: 50 Points

- Sketch up a 10 frame storyboard (25 pts.) based on the five minute framework. It should illustrate your facts and how you will present them in the video—you will not be improvising this!
- Daily effort using rubric below (25 pts.)

Level 4: 50 Points

- Write a script (25 pts.) based on the five minute framework—you will not be improvising the speaking lines!
- Daily effort using rubric below (25 pts.)

Level 5: 50 Points

- Organize (5 pts.) props, determine locations, practice characters
- Rehearse (5 pts.) the script completely several times without a camera
- Film (15 pts.) the movie and all needed footage with camera
- Daily effort using rubric below (25 pts.)

Level 6: 50 Points

- Create original music (25 pts.) and / or sound effects to use somewhere in the movie
- Daily effort using rubric below (25 pts. each day)

Level 7: 50 Points

- Edit (25 pts.) and compile all parts of the movie in Mixcraft, GarageBand, iMovie, or Windows Movie Maker
- Daily effort using rubric below (25 pts. each day)

Level 8: 50 Points

- Overflow day—finish extra work
- Finish editing (10 pts.) in your video editing program
- Watch the movie as a group all the way through to make any last minute changes
- Add titles and credits (15 pts.)
- Daily effort using rubric below (25 pts.)

Level 9

- Movie party!

Effort / Creativity / Focus Grading Rubric

0–5 points ....I did almost nothing and put forth extremely low effort.

6–10 points ....I did a little more than the minimum and put forth just a little effort.

11–15 points ......I worked with average creativity and put forth average effort.

16–20 points ......I did great work, had great focus, and put forth great effort.

21–25 points ......I did top-notch work, showed superior creativity, and put forth excellent effort.

no website

NAME_____

Level 1: 50 Points

____/5 points.....Brainstorm topics (5 pts.) with to decide on subject matter.

____/5 points.....Brainstorm how to present (5 pts.) the movie

____/15 points...Create a five minute framework (15 pts.) / skeleton

____/25 points...Daily effort—see rubric for levels (25 pts.)

Level 2: 50 Points

____/20 points...Gather facts and do research (25 pts.)—at minimum *10 to 20* facts

____/5 points.....Create characters if you are not playing yourself in the movie

____/25 points...Daily effort—see rubric for levels (25 pts.)

Level 3: 50 Points

____/25 points...Sketch up storyboard/script (25 pts.)—use 5 minute framework, details *facts*

____/25 points...Daily effort—see rubric for levels (25 pts.)

Level 4: 50 Points

____/25 points...Write a script (25 pts.) based on the five minute framework

____/25 points...Daily effort—see rubric for levels (25 pts.)

Level 5: 50 Points

____/5 points.....Organize (5 pts.) props, determine locations, practice characters

____/5 points.....Rehearse (5 pts.) the script completely several times without a camera

____/15 points...Film (15 pts.) the movie and all needed footage with camera

____/25 points...Daily effort—see rubric for levels (25 pts.)

Level 6: 50 Points

____/25 points...Create original music (25 pts.) and/or sound effects

____/25 points...Daily effort—see rubric for levels (25 pts.)

Level 7: 50 Points

____/25 points...Edit (25 pts.) the movie, music, and all the parts together

____/25 points...Daily effort—see rubric for levels (25 pts.)

Level 8: 50 Points

____/10 points...Add a transition or visual effect (10 pts.) in your video editor

____/15 points...Add titles and credits (15 pts.)

____/0 points.....Watch the movie all the way through

____/25 points...Daily effort—see rubric for levels (25 pts.)

____/400 pts......*Project total*

Three things I learned from this project were:

Figure II.6

MOVIE SOUNDTRACK AND SCORING

YOUR MISSION

Choose a short video clip (less than 5 minutes) and create your own soundtrack to replace the original audio. The focus of this project is the creation of a soundtrack, as opposed to the next project which is based on the use of sound effects.

For this project, you will need to download an interesting short video clip that inspires you to write a new music soundtrack to accompany it. You might use a short cartoon, an action scene from a movie (like a car chase or fight), a commercial, or anything that is visually interesting. YouTube is a fantastic source, and there are several websites that will allow you to download video clips from YouTube. Once you have your clip, you're ready to rock!

- Sound mapping (50 points): Use the storyboard template on page 138 to create a timeline of all visual events and the music you want to accompany them. You must write music in at least two different styles or emotions for the clip. Some videos (like cartoons) may demand several styles within the space of just a few seconds!

- Sound tracking Part One—Style /Emotion #1 (75 points): Write music to accompany the first part of the video. What music would fit best with what you see? How can the music enhance the visual action?

- Sound tracking Part Two—Style /Emotion #2 (75 points): Write music in a different style or emotion to accompany the second part of the video. What music would fit best with what you see? How can the music enhance the visual action?

- Sound editing / arrangement / mixdown (50 points): Load, assemble, and edit the music and the video in Mixcraft , GarageBand, or iMovie. Move them around on the timeline to get precise timing with video. Export the final blended movie and watch it to check for accuracy of timing. Make adjustments as necessary.

- Creative power (50 points): Each day, evaluate yourself on a 25 point scale using the rubric below. How much did you focus, concentrate, and put creative energy and spirit into the project? How deliberate and directed was your work? How strong was your work ethic? If the project goes beyond two days, continue to use the 25 point daily rubric—just add that to the total points possible for the project.

Total: 300 points

0–5 points ....I did almost nothing and put forth extremely low effort.

6–10 points ....I did a little more than the minimum and put forth just a little effort.

11–15 points ......I worked with average creativity and put forth average effort.

16–20 points ......I did great work, had great focus, and put forth great effort.

21–25 points ......I did top-notch work, showed superior creativity, and put forth excellent effort.

Figure II.7

SOUND EFFECTS/FOLEY USING MIXCRAFT/ GARAGEBAND

YOUR MISSION

Choose a short, one-minute video clip and create your own soundtrack, sound effects, Foley, and overdubbed vocals to replace the original audio using Mixcraft or GarageBand. The focus of this project is the use of sound effects, as opposed to the previous project which was based on the creation of a soundtrack.

For this project, you will need to download an interesting short video clip that inspires you to change its audio track. You might use a short cartoon, an action scene from a movie (like a car chase or fight), a commercial, or anything that is visually interesting. YouTube is a fantastic source, and there are several websites that will allow you to download video clips from YouTube. Once you have your clip, you're ready to rock!

Sound Mapping: 50 points

• Use the Storyboard template on page 138 to create a timeline of all visual events and the sounds you want to accompany them. Write out each sound effect and the exact second it occurs.

Sound Tracking: 50 points

• Find music to accompany the video—even better if you produce and write it yourself! What music would fit best with what you see? Maybe even choose music that would

deliberately not fit, to create a humorous video!

Sound Procurement: 50 points

• Find and download each sound effect and/ or use a mic to record special Foley effects. Use sound effects sites online (Freesound. org, SoundDogs, and so on) or use your imagination and bring in things from home to create the sounds you need.

Sound Editing/Arrangement: 50 Points

• Edit (trim) and assemble sounds in Mixcraft /GarageBand and line them up with the timeline giving close attention to accuracy. Each sound should get its own track. (You may end up with dozens of tracks, so use names to help distinguish them.) Move them around on the timeline to get precise timing with video.

Final Mixdown: 50 points

• Export the final blended movie and watch it to check for accuracy of timing. Make adjustments as necessary.

Creative Power: 50 points

• Use the rubric below. How much did you focus, concentrate, and put creative energy and spirit into the project? How deliberate and directed was your work? How strong was your work ethic?

• If the project goes beyond two days, evaluate yourself on a 25 point scale daily using the rubric below—then add that to the total points for the project.

Total = 300 points

Effort/Creativity/Focus Grading Rubric

0–5 points ....I did almost nothing and put forth extremely low effort.

6–10 points ....I did a little more than the

minimum and put forth just a little effort.

11–15 points ......I worked with average creativity and put forth average effort.

16–20 points ......I did great work, had great focus, and put forth great effort.

21–25 points ......I did top-notch work, showed superior creativity, and put forth excellent effort.

Figure II.8

FREEDOM OF SPEECH

YOUR MISSION

Manipulate a famous speech to create new meanings that the original speaker never intended.

Resource

www.americanrhetoric.com √

1. Visit the American Rhetoric website to choose a speech you can download.

2. Right-click the file, choose Save As, and download the MP3 into a new folder called Freedom of Speech.

3. Click on the speech's title. Doing so will take you to a transcript of the speech you just downloaded. Copy and paste this into Microsoft Word and save that version in your Freedom of Speech folder as well.

4. Select any *one* minute of the speech to work with as base material. Use Word to edit and rearrange word order in that minute to create new meaning. You may also grab words from other areas of the speech to combine with your base material.

5. Be creative in your manipulations. Make the speech funnier, make words repeat, omit important words, and so on.

6. You must make at least *ten* edits. The focus is on meaning, not on effects (such as reverb, distortion, and so on). Map out your plan for the cut-ups.

7. Use Mixcraft, GarageBand, or Audacity cut-and-paste tools to re-create the speech, manipulating the MP3 you downloaded.

8. Finally, add a simple drum loop or a quiet musical groove to accompany the speech.

9. Balance the volume levels in your speech against the music.

Grading

60 points ....Ten edits/changes (6 pts. each)

25 points ....Personal effort, using the Effort/Creativity/Focus grading rubric

15 points ....Addition of a musical groove

100 points ....*Totally awesome!*

Effort/Creativity/Focus Grading Rubric

0–5 points ....I did almost nothing and put forth extremely low effort.

6–10 points ....I did a little more than the minimum and put forth just a little effort.

11–15 points ......I worked with average creativity and put forth average effort.

16–20 points ......I did great work, had great focus, and put forth great effort.

21–25 points ......I did top-notch work, showed superior creativity, and put forth excellent effort.

Storyboard Template

Title:_____   Storyboard Sheet #_____

Shot #_____   Shot #_____
Description/Dialogue:_____   Description/Dialogue:_____
_____   _____
_____   _____

Shot #_____   Shot #_____
Description/Dialogue:_____   Description/Dialogue:_____
_____   _____
_____   _____

Shot #_____   Shot #_____
Description/Dialogue:_____   Description/Dialogue:_____
_____   _____
_____   _____

Music Research Notes

Fact 1	
Fact 2	
Fact 3	
Fact 4	
Fact 5	
Fact 6	
Fact 7	
Fact 8	
Fact 9	
Fact 10	

Music Research Notes

Figure II.9

GOANIMATE.COM

YOUR MISSION

Create a two- to three-minute entertaining animation that educates viewers about a musical topic.

Resource

www.GoAnimate.com

Go Animate can be used for free but the number of scenes, characters, props, etc. are extremely limited. They offer commercial and personal pricing plans—I recommend getting a quarterly subscription for personal use. It is extremely cheap and gives an educational / student user many options for creativity!

Step 1: Understanding GoAnimate. com

• Log in to the site.

• Watch tutorials.

• Start a video from scratch!

Step 2: Research and Planning

• What are you going to be teaching viewers? Choose your topic and research it.

• The topic *must* be about music!

• Use the Music Research Template on page 139. It will help you to research and list facts or interesting things you would like to share about the topic.

• Organize your facts into groups and choose a way to present them in a particular order.

Step 3: Storyboarding

• Use the Storyboard template on page 138 to create a two-page storyboard. Each square should represent approximately 10 seconds (2 minutes total).

• Sketch your scenes and characters, and identify where and how your facts will be presented.

• Add some anchoring lines of dialog / text.

Step 4: Animating

• Base your animation on your storyboard, and pay close attention to requirements listed below.

Grading

60 points ....Complete a storyboard (5 points per block).

50 points ....Teach at least 10 facts (5 points per fact).

40 points ....Complete an animation that is at least 2 minutes long (5 points per 15 seconds).

15 points ....Use at least three different scenes /backgrounds (5 points each).

15 points ....Rearrange one of those scenes.

15 points ....Use at least three different characters.

15 points ....All three characters must move (5 points per character).

15 points ....All three characters must talk (5 points per character).

15 points ....Use at least three different props (5 points each).

15 points ....Use at least three FX (5 points each).

15 points ....Use at least three sound effects.

20 points ....Use at least two different songs (10 points each).

10 points ....Use one "thought" bubble.

300 points ....*Totally awesome!*

You will also be given a daily effort grade of up to 25 points per day using the standard scale below.

Effort / Creativity / Focus Grading Rubric

0–5 points ....I did almost nothing and put forth extremely low effort.

6–10 points ....I did a little more than the minimum and put forth just a little effort.

11–15 points ......I worked with average creativity and put forth average effort.

16–20 points ......I did great work, had great focus, and put forth great effort.

21–25 points ......I did top-notch work, showed superior creativity, and put forth excellent effort.

Figure II.10

MUSIC TECHNOLOGY STATIONS

YOUR MISSION

Move from station to station and engage with music technology in different and fun ways!

You will be given 10 minutes at each station. When it is time to move to the next station, you will have to move regardless of whether you are finished with your current assignment. If there is an even number of students in your class, you should partner up with someone to "travel" with. If there is an odd number of students, your teacher can participate with a partner.

STATION 1: MP3 LISTENING

Assignment
Listen to two songs from an iPod / MP3 player (yours or a friend's). At least one song must be one you've never heard before.

Assessment
Answer in complete sentences for *at least one* of the songs you listened to.

1. What is the song about?

2. How does the song make you feel?

Write or rewrite any portion of the song. (Usually rewriting the chorus is the easiest.)

STATION 2: MUSICAL WEBSITE 1, CLASS COMPOSITION

Assignment
• Set up two computers to create two different songs.

• If you are the first group, you must create some kind of basic groove for a class song that is approximately one to two minutes long.

• If you are the second group, you must in

• some way add/subtract/change/remix the music your classmates have written. You may *not* start over from scratch.

Assessment
You must do each of the following steps:

1. Listen to the entire song.

2. Figure out what is good (keep).

3. Figure out what is bad (delete).

4. Figure out what can be changed (remix), using effects, reverses, extend, and so on.

5. Figure out what to add. Pick your own loops and samples that match!

STATION 3: ARTICLE/MAGAZINE READING

Assignment
Pick any short article out of music magazines like Rolling Stone, Spin, or The Source. You have only two minutes to pick the article, so don't be too choosy.

Assessment
Read the article and then share with your partner what the article was about. Then have your partner do the same. Write down in complete sentences what your partner says about his or her article.

• What was your partner's article about?

• What would your partner do differently if he or she had written the article?

• If your partner could get paid $500 to write an article about music, what specifically would it be about? Why?

STATION 4: YOUR CHOICE OF AWESOME MUSIC LINKS, PART 1

Assignment
Choose a link from the long list provided. For this station, you may also want to check out the larger list of links available on the companion site to this book.

You must explore it in enough depth to be able to learn something from it.

Even if the site is geared toward elementary-school kids, you must try to find the musical value and potential in it.

Assessment
Site visited:

If you were the teacher, how would you use this website in a lesson plan? Write a short assignment for a class of students using this site.

STATION 5: KEYBOARDS

Assignment
Play the keyboard (at least two should be set up). Try to pick out a song you are familiar with. Try switching the instrument sounds and explore some interesting ways to use the keyboard.

Assessment
Demonstrate to your partner one neat thing you accomplished or learned about the keyboard, and teach your partner how to do it as well. Answer in complete sentences.

• What did your partner teach you to do?

• What did you teach your partner?

STATION 6: SONG-LYRIC WRITING

Assignment
Work with a partner to write lyrics to a song. You may choose any topic.

Assessment
You must write at least one verse and one chorus, but you may write more.

VERSE 1

1.

2.

3.

4.

CHORUS

1.

2.

3.

4.

VERSE 2

1.

2.

3.

4.

STATION 7: YOUR CHOICE OF AWESOME MUSIC LINKS, PART 2

Assignment

Choose a link from the long list provided. For this station, you may want to check out the larger list of free links available on the companion site to this book.

It must be different from the site you previously visited. You must explore it in enough depth to be able to learn something from it.

Even if the site is geared toward elementary-school kids, you must try to find the musical value and potential in it.

Assessment

Site visited:

If you were the teacher, how would you use this in a lesson plan? Write a short assignment for a class of students using this site.

MUSIC LINKS FOR STATIONS 4 AND 7

Composing/Notation

http://www.iknowthat.com/com/L3?Area=Music *(computer)*

http://www.creatingmusic.com/ *(computer)*

http://www.jamstudio.com/ *(computer)*

http://www.philtulga.com/ *instrument projects*

http://inudge.net/ *(computer)*

http://www.incredibox.fr/ *(computer no ipad)*

Instruments/Composers

http://www.sphinxkids.org *× (computer)*

http://www.classicsforkids.com *(computers)*

http://www.artsalive.ca/en/mus/(composers, instruments) *✗*

http://www.nyphilkids.org/games/main.phtml *(computers)*

http://www.dsokids.com (a few games) *(computers)*

http://www.sfskids.org (instruments, composing) *(computers)*

http://tinyurl.com/ezgu6 (Carnegie hall) *✗*

Instruments (Literally)

http://www.kenbrashear.com/ *✗*

http://www.thevirtualpiano.com *?*

http://www.bluelaserdesign.com/idjturntables.htm *?*

http://www.turntables.de/ *✗*

http://worteldrie.com/WD-1/index.html *✗*

Music Theory

http://www.musicards.net/ *✓*

http://www.netrover.com/~kingskid/piano/piano.html *✗*

http://musicracer.com/ *✗*

http://www.musictheory.net/

http://teoria.com *Computers*

http://www.emusictheory.com/practice.html *download*

http://www.ossmann.com/bigears/(ear training)

Super-Duper Resources

http://www.childrensmusicworkshop.com *(computers)*

http://www.musicoutfitters.com/children.htm

http://www.mtna.org/Resources/
WebsitesforKids/tabid/320/Default.aspx

http://www.ababasoft.com/music/

http://www.childrensmusic.org/ *(elementary)*

http://www.theradiohour.net

Awesome Gaming Resources

http://www.flashmusicgames.com/

http://www.dailygames.com/musicgames.html

http://www.primarygames.com/arcade/music.
htm

http://www.oyunlar1.com/musicgames.asp

Remixing

http://www.soundation.com

http://www.ccmixter.org

http://www.youtubemultiplier.com/   *cool*

http://www.partycloud.fm/ *(computer)*

Actual Instruments

http://www.rinki.net/pekka/monkey/#

http://www.audiotool.com

http://www.onemotion.com/flash/drum-
machine/

http://www.buttonbeats.com *(computers)*

http://sequencer.sodah.de/ *(computer)*

Super-Fun Stuff

http://lab.andre-michelle.com/

http://www.bbc.co.uk/arts/multimedia/
soundkit2/

http://jlapotre.free.fr/bpoem/bpoem.html

http://www.skop.com/brucelee/index.htm

Figure III.1

PART 3

Music Tech in the Real World

In Part 3, you'll complete rigorous, long-term projects relevant to your interests. For example, if you're interested in English, you might create multimedia storytelling projects. If you're interested in sports, you might provide a vehicle to write music for gaming events. If you're interested in science or biology, you might explore musical-therapy applications in the medical field. If you're interested in social studies, you might research cultural groups inspired by music made with technology. If you're interested in art, you might work with video/music installations or performance-art pieces. If you're interested in computer science or mathematics, you might explore writing music-making apps.

The skills you acquire in Part 3 will develop your creative artistry and expression, and open your mind to new avenues of music-making within your own world.

Goals for Part 3

- Study how musical gadgets such as iPods work
- Create multimedia stories
- Build simple electronic-music machines
- Study sampling and copyright law
- Make a documentary on the history of recorded music and recording companies
- Report about music's influence on subcultures (such as EDM, rave/house, goth, industrial, rap)
- Create mood music for athletes and crowds at a sporting event
- Report on recording institutes and radio schools
- Create music for video games
- Create musical apps for smartphones

Figure I.1

PART 1

FUNDAMENTALS

Part 1 of *Music Tech 101* covers the fundamentals of music technology and gives you the opportunity to create, share, discuss, read, write about, and listen to music made with technology. You'll actively use technology to explore these elements as you investigate a broad range of topics. We will focus primarily on the history and possible futures of technology and its impact on the world of music. Part 1 covers topics like audio editing, sequencing software, remixing, sound systems, the modern music business, studio recording, synthesizers, copyright law, DJing, recording media, electric guitars, video-game music, and other contemporary themes.

Goals for Part 1
- Write your own rap
- Create beats on the computer
- Make a radio commercial
- Remix songs
- Learn about the modern music business
- Create your own DJ mixtape
- Analyze how your favorite song was made
- Write music online
- Create your own record label

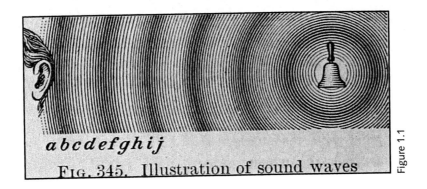

abcdefghij

FIG. 345. Illustration of sound waves

Figure 1.1

UNIT 1
THE SCIENCE OF SOUND

UNIT READING

Studying the physics of sound is a fundamental place to get started understanding concepts. in music technology. Knowing how sound waves work provides the basis for thinking about early synthesizers, electricity, and the beginning of electronic music.

SOUND WAVES

First, let's start by understanding the *electromagnetic spectrum*. There are two types of electromagnetic waves: *mechanical* (which must travel through a medium) and *electromagnetic* (which can travel through a vacuum). The lowest and largest electromagnetic waves, with the smallest amount of energy, are sound waves—while radio and television waves are a bit more intense. Microwaves, mobile phones, radars, and remote controls occupy the next few tiers of energy, followed by visible light. X-rays and gamma rays occupy the most energetic segment of the spectrum.

Frequency

The *frequency* of a sound wave describes the number of times it vibrates per second. A popular reference frequency is A = 440 hertz, which is the A above middle C on the piano keyboard. For this particular A, the piano string vibrates at 440 *hertz* (cycles per second, abbreviated as *Hz*). Piano tuners use this tone as a reference for tuning a piano—doubling the number to 880Hz produces the A note one octave (eight notes) higher, and 220Hz is one octave lower. Frequencies are important to understand because they ultimately indicate how high or how low a particular note is—an important concept for synthesizers, since they produce notes with electricity. (We will be discussing synthesizers later in this unit.) Humans can hear sounds within the range of 20Hz to 20,000Hz (or, 20kHz). Once sounds are released into the atmosphere, the particles push against each other, travel through the air, and reach our eardrums, which vibrate at the same rate. Our ears then convert these vibrations into electrical signals, which our brains perceive as sound. The speed of sound changes depending upon what material it travels through. When a supersonic jet reaches Mach 1, it will be going faster than the speed of sound through air, which is 768 miles per hour.

Ultrasound

Extremely high frequencies above our hearing range are called *ultrasound* and have many practical applications apart from music. Animals, such as bats and dolphins, use ultrasound for echolocation to detect their prey. Medical sonography uses ultrasound to help visualize parts of the body, including muscles, organs, and babies in the womb. And ultrasonic cleaners can get rid of tiny particles of dirt on jewelry or medical equipment.

Infrasound

Extremely low frequencies below our hearing range are called *infrasound* and have frequent occurrences in both the natural and industrial world. Earthquakes, volcanic activity, and heavy surf all produce infrasound and can be sensed a few miles away by animals and instruments, such as a seismograph, to warn of possible danger. Some animals, such as elephants and alligators, use infrasound to communicate with each other over the distance of several miles. And some factory equipment and heating systems produce infrasound at high decibels when in operation. These sounds are very low, often undetectable by the human ear, but they have been known to cause illness and headaches with workers.

Decibel

The *decibel* (dB) level of a sound wave describes the intensity of the sound's frequency at a given distance—or, more simply put, a sound's volume. Normal speech falls around 60dB to 70dB, a lawn mower outputs around 100dB, sounds start to feel painful at about 125dB, and hearing loss can occur at around 180dB. It is even possible to break a drinking glass using only the human voice—if the sound is concentrated onto a very narrow area, the decibel level is high enough, and the singer matches the exact resonant frequency of the glass. There was an episode of the TV show *MythBusters* dedicated to this experiment.

Waveforms

Sound waves can travel in different forms. Their cycles may vary in shape, and in turn the resultant sounds of different waves can be radically dissimilar. *Sawtooth-shaped waves* produce the bright, brassy timbre of a trumpet. *Sine waves,* with their gentle and even slopes, produce a sound similar to a flute. *Square waves* sound like wind instruments, such as a clarinet. Early electronic keyboard instruments, like the Minimoog, used these different waveforms to imitate the sounds of acoustic instruments, though their tones nevertheless remained distinctly electronic. These early electronic keyboards created, modified, and combined various waveforms to generate new sounds never before heard! This is why many keyboards were referred to as *synthesizers*.

Acoustics

The study of the way sound travels is called *acoustics*. It's important to understand this science, especially when designing recording studios and concert halls. In a recording studio, walls may intersect at odd angles (to prevent the reflection of sound), or they may be extra thick and covered with soundproofing material (to prevent sounds from entering or escaping the environment). This causes a room to be acoustically "dead" and is advantageous in a studio because it enables the recording engineer to capture a very clean, isolated portrait of instruments or singers. In a concert hall, sound needs to travel some distance to reach all members of the audience, yet the hall cannot be constructed in a way that allows echoing sound to interfere with the clarity of what is heard. As a result, acoustic technicians, or acousticians, must understand mathematically and architecturally how to construct various spaces to suit the room's purpose.

RADIO WAVES

A final topic for this unit is radio, and specifically, *radio waves*. Radio originated as a wireless form of communication around the beginning of the 1900s. There are four basic kinds of radio transmission: *AM* (amplitude modulation), *FM* (frequency modulation), *HD* (high definition), and *satellite*. Each of these carries music on radio waves that constantly bombard our bodies from every direction. However, to detect the waves, you must use the right kind of antenna and receiver. It's pretty amazing to think that radio enables invisible music to travel through the air!

Most radio waves are used for one-way communication. However, *ham radio* (amateur radio) is intended for private use and can support long-distance communication among multiple parties, while *CB* (citizens band) radio is used for localized communication between individuals.

Figure 1.2 Vocalists Joan Weldon and Byron Palmer

Figure 1.3 Laboratory ultrasonic bath

Figure 1.4 *Tsunami* by Hokusai, 1826

STUDENT WORKSHEET

1. What term describes the number of vibrations per second of a frequency?

2. What is the range of frequencies the human ear can detect?

3. A man's voice has a certain frequency range. A woman's voice occupies another frequency range. Which voice vibrates at a faster rate?

   (See Figure 1.2)

4. Name the term for extremely high frequencies.

5. What animal can detect the highest frequency sounds?

6. What practical purpose do ultrasonic waves serve? *(See Figure 1.3)*

7. Name the term for extremely low frequencies.

8. What animal can detect the lowest frequency sounds?

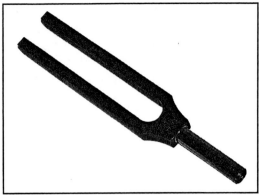
Figure 1.5 Tuning fork

Figure 1.6 VU decibel meter

Figure 1.7 A U.S. Navy jet breaks the sound barrier

Figure 1.8 Resonant frequencies can break glass

9. What practical purpose do infrasonic waves serve? *(See Figure 1.4)*

10. Music is based on blending different frequencies. If a tuning fork vibrates at 1000Hz, at what rate would another fork need to vibrate to sound an octave (eight notes) lower? *(See Figure 1.5)*

11. Describe in simple terms how your ears function.

12. What do decibels (dB) measure? *(See Figure 1.6)*

13. At what approximate decibel level do the following occur?

    a. Quiet conversation

    b. A power mower

    c. Pain

    d. Actual hearing loss

14. The speed of sound changes depending upon the material it travels through. When a supersonic jet reaches Mach 1, it will be going faster than the speed of sound through air. How fast is that? *(See Figure 1.7)*

Figure 1.9 Acoustics of a large concert hall

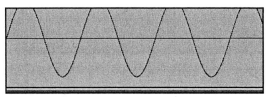
Figure 1.10 50Hz sine wave

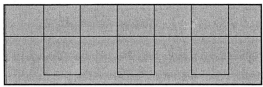
Figure 1.11 50Hz square wave

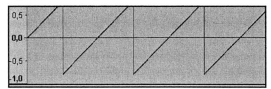
Figure 1.12 50Hz sawtooth wave

Figure 1.13 An antique radio

15. How can a singer break a drinking glass with his or her voice? *(See Figure 1.8)*

16. What are acoustics and why are they important in studios and concert halls? *(See Figure 1.9)*

17. Early synthesizers produced different kinds of sound waves in an effort to imitate actual musical instruments. Name *two* types of waves and the musical instruments they sound closest to. *(See Figures 1.10–1.12)*

18. What does it mean to synthesize something?

19. Radio was invented in the early 1900s. Name *three* kinds of radio transmission. *(See Figure 1.13)*

20. What is ham radio?

UNIT PROJECT

YOUR MISSION

Write a song or rap by yourself or with a partner that describes something you learned from Unit 1. Use the WD-1 website (www.worteldrie.com/WD-1) to provide the music. You can write music first and then lyrics, or lyrics and then music.

Resource

www.worteldrie.com/WD-1   ✗

Music

Follow these steps to help with writing music for your Unit Project:

1. Go to the WD-1 website: www.worteldrie.com/WD-1.

2. Choose a style of music you like and a beat that you can write lyrics to.

3. Use the keyboard and mouse to "play" the WD-1 live, and try to develop a song.

4. The song must use the following format. Use the keys to play some funky stuff!

- Intro
- Verse 1
- Chorus
- Verse 2
- Chorus
- Outro

5. Practice the song. If you need to, take notes on which keys you are pressing.

6. Open Mixcraft, GarageBand, Audacity, or another recording software, and record your song.

Lyrics

Use the following guide to help with writing lyrics for your Unit Project:

- Verse 1: 4 lines
- Chorus: 4 lines
- Verse 2: 4 lines
- Chorus: Repeated
- The lyrics should rhyme and can be spoken, rapped, or sung.
- The lyrics should include five topics or facts from the notes of this unit.
- You can sneak facts in any way you'd like—be creative!
- Work quickly, efficiently, and smartly, since you'll have limited time to work on this song.
- Create a solid beginning and ending for extra polish. The total time of the song should be less than three minutes.

Grading

25 points ....Use the WD-1 interatively, with changes /builds /breakdowns and so on.

25 points ....Include five topics /facts in the lyrics (5 points each).

25 points ....Proper structure:

>   Intro ....2.5 points
>   Verse 1 ....5 points
>   Chorus ....5 points
>   Verse 2 ....5 points
>   Chorus ....5 points
>   Outro ....2.5 points

25 points ....Record the music and lyrics in Mixcraft, GarageBand, or Audacity and save them as an MP3 to share.

_____

100 points ....*Totally awesome!*

Extra Credit

+20 points ....Perform it live with your partner in class.

+20 points ....Use some kind of effects on the song after it has been recorded.

+5 points ....Write an additional verse (5 points for each additional verse you write).

MASTER PROJECT SHEET

YOUR MISSION

You will be completing at least five large projects in this course. They will help you to explore the intersection of music and technology as it applies to individualized goals within various discipline areas. The projects will develop your creative artistry and open your mind to new avenues of self-expression. Your education = your choice.

Choose (25 Points)

- A main subject (example: English)
- A specific topic (example: children's books)
- A project (example: record narrated words, music, and sound FX for Tikki Tikki Tembo)
- A technology tool (example: Mixcraft or GarageBand)
- A method of final delivery (example: create an MP3 for others to listen to)

Design and Plan (75 Points)

1. Write a set of three learning goals for the project (25 points). For example:

   - I will learn how to write a soundtrack in Mixcraft/GarageBand.
   - I will learn how to find sound FX online and use them in a story.
   - I will learn how to assemble music, narration, and sound FX tracks into a seamless flow of a single MP3 using Mixcraft/GarageBand.

2. Write an outline for the project or the details of your plans (50 points). For example:

   - Step 1: Design, set goals, plan, outline.
   - Step 2: Choose a children's book. Plan vocal inflection/how to read it.
   - Step 3: Record my vocal narration of the book into Mixcraft/GarageBand.
   - Step 4: Find 15 sound effects online

that I can use for my recording.
   - Step 5: Write music using loops on Mixcraft/GarageBand.
   - Step 6: Mix down the music, narration, and sound FX within Mixcraft/GarageBand.
   - Step 7: Share with the class.
   - Step 8: Review and grade the work.

Research (50 Points)

- Find reading sources about your topic (example: go to the library & check out Tikki Tikki Tembo).
- Take notes about your topic if necessary (example: write down some websites with sound FX and plan how long your Mixcraft/GarageBand music should last or if it should change mood mid-story).
- Learn how to use your technology tool (example: learn about recording in Mixcraft/GarageBand).
- Make sure you become an expert in all facets of your project—be thorough!

Create/Work (250 Points)

50 points per day, 5 days max, for a total of 250 points. If your project takes fewer than five or longer than five days, simply divide the 250 points among the number of days for your daily effort grade.

- Follow your plan in order.
- Experiment a bit with your project and be flexible.
- Be creative and express yourself.

Share and Educate (50 Points)

1. Present your project to the class when you are finished (example: play the MP3).

2. Give the students something to think about. Ask them at least three questions pertaining to your presentation/topic/project. For example: What kinds of sound FX did you

hear as the MP3 was playing? How did the music I wrote contribute to the story? How could I have taken this project to the next level?

3. Take both compliments and constructive criticism gracefully.

4. Field all comments and questions, and answer them accurately.

Review (50 Points)

1. Write five short paragraphs as a written review of your project.

   - Paragraph 1: Evaluate/describe what you did well.
   - Paragraph 2: Evaluate/describe what you could've improved upon.
   - Paragraph 3: Describe what you learned from the project.
   - Paragraph 4: Describe what you liked and/or disliked about the project.
   - Paragraph 5: Evaluate/describe the class input and reaction to the project.

2. Tally up your total points/grade in detail and describe why you deserve it!

MAIN SUBJECTS

You must pick five subjects over the semester—four different and one repeatable. Choose your five from the following:

- English
- Sciences/math/technology
- Politics/law
- Social studies/foreign studies
- Sports
- Education
- Music
- Art
- Entertainment

Specific Topic Ideas: English

You must pick five different topics over the semester.

- Creating multimedia stories (with music, sound FX, pictures)
- Writing soundtracks to a story (varies according to storyline)
- Writing educational stories about music
- Music journalism—reviewing and reporting
- Reading stories about music
- Writing a radio program
- Creating parodies
- Working on your own original idea

Specific Topic Ideas: Sciences/Math/Technology

You must pick five different topics over the semester.

- Creating environmentalism awareness
- Substituting a song's lyrics with science facts
- Creating simple electronic music machines (circuitry)
- Studying psychological effects of various musical genres
- Examining music therapy in senior homes or medical applications
- Studying how musical gadgets work (iPods, keyboards, software, and so on)
- Examining the Internet's effect on music distribution and creation
- Working with computers or software that make music (Max)
- Working on your own original idea

Specific Topic Ideas: Politics/Law

You must pick five different topics over the semester.

- Writing or rewriting song lyrics pertaining to a political topic

- Reporting on activist music (hippies, folk, political punk, and so on)
- Examining copyright and copyright law
- Considering freedom of speech in music
- Examining music in the military
- Considering entertainment law
- Working on your own original idea

Specific Topic Ideas: Social Studies / Foreign Studies

You must pick five different topics over the semester.

- Studying subcultures centered around genres of music (EDM, rave / house, rap)
- Examining music and animals
- Studying music from particular cities or countries
- Considering histories of particular musical traditions / cultures
- Discussing the history of recorded music and / or recording companies
- Studying concert crowd behavior
- Examining dancing styles and their origins
- Working on your own original ideaSports
- Studying TV bumper music
- Creating short mood-music for live sporting events (crowd participation)
- Studying the psychological effects of music on athletes
- Working on your own original idea

Specific Topic Ideas: Education

You must pick five different topics over the semester.

- Studying techniques for music education (Orff, Kodaly, and so on)
- Examining music tech programs in the U.S. (high school or collegiate)
- Considering music's influence on learning or

study

- Learning about music therapy techniques for special-needs kids
- Examining reports on recording institutes and / or radio broadcasting schools
- Working on your own original idea

Specific Topic Ideas: Music

You must pick five different topics over the semester.

- Touring
- Recording
- Marketing
- Examining the art of performing / entertainment methods
- Discussing Music 3.0
- Providing software / hardware title overviews
- Learning about music for video games
- Consider music about particular topics
- Working on your own original idea

Specific Topic Ideas: Art

You must pick five different topics over the semester.

- Considering graphic arts / animation and music
- Putting together slides of original art with a soundtrack
- Creating public art installations (displayed in a school hallway)
- Considering art about music (concert flyers, album covers, and so on)
- Examining digital art
- Working on your own original idea
- Specific Topic Ideas: Entertainment
- Discussing sound systems (auto, home, concert arenas)
- Considering film-music studies / soundtracking

- Examining commercial music
- Discussing Foley / sound FX
- Learning about iPad or iPod musical apps
- Discussing musical video games
- Working on your own original idea

A Technology Tool

You must pick five different methods—one for each project.

- Software (example: GarageBand, Pro Tools, Audacity, Mixcraft, Soundation, Reason, ACID, ReBirth, and so on)
- Hardware (keyboard, drum machine, iPod, iPad, Flip camera, electric guitar, interface, and so on)
- Nonmusical software (PowerPoint, CamStudio, Movie Maker, Paint, Scratch game programmer, Photoshop, and so on)
- The Internet and particular websites

A Method of Final Delivery

You must pick three different methods—two are repeatable.

- Live performance
- PowerPoint / Prezi
- Digital song file (MP3)
- Video
- Website / blog
- App or multimedia software program
- Hardware
- Digital artwork based on music (flyer, digital comic, animation, and so on)
- Digital book
- Art installation

MASTER PLANNING GRADING SHEET

Choose (_/25 points)

- A main subject:
- A specific topic:
- A project:
- A technology tool:
- A method of final delivery:

DESIGN AND PLAN

- Write a set of three learning goals for the project (_/25 points)
  1. I will learn:
  2. I will learn:
  3. I will learn:
- Write an outline for the project/details of your plans (_/50 points)
  1. Step 1:
  2. Step 2:
  3. Step 3:
  4. Step 4:
  5. Step 5:
  6. Step 6:
  7. Step 7:
  8. Step 8:

Research (_/50 points)

- Find reading sources about your topic.
- Take notes about your topic if necessary.
- Learn about how to use your technology tool.
- Make sure you become an expert in all facets of your project—be complete and thorough!

Create/Work (_/250 points)

If your project takes fewer than five or longer than five days, simply divide the 250 points among the number of days for your daily effort grade.

- Follow your plan in order.
- Experiment a bit with your project and be flexible.
- Be creative and express yourself.
  1. Day 1:_/50
  2. Day 2:_/50
  3. Day 3:_/50
  4. Day 4:_/50
  5. Day 5:_/50

Share and Educate (_/50 points)

- Present your project to the class when you're finished.
- Give the students something to think about—ask them at least three questions pertaining to your presentation / topic / project.
- Take both compliments and constructive criticism gracefully.
- Field all comments and questions accurately.

Review (_/50 points)

- Write five short paragraphs as a written review of your project:
  1. Paragraph 1: Evaluate/describe what you did well.
  2. Paragraph 2: Evaluate/describe what you could've improved upon.
  3. Paragraph 3: Describe what you liked about the project.
  4. Paragraph 4: Describe what you disliked about the project.
  5. Paragraph 5: Evaluate/describe the class input and reaction to the project.
- Each paragraph is worth 10 points.
- Tally up your grade and describe why you deserve it!

Final Grade..........._/500

INDEX
PHOTO CREDITS

PART 1

Figure I.1—Title: Minimoog (Buffalo Museum of Science)
Web address: http://en.wikipedia.org/wiki/Moog_
synthesizer#mediaviewer/File:Minimoog_%28Buffalo_Museum_of_
Science%29.jpg
Author: Alex Harden
Author web address: http://www.flickr.com/people/24396426@N00
Licensed Under: CC by 2.0
License Web Address: http://creativecommons.org/licenses/by/2.0

Unit 1

Figure 1.1—Title: Image from page 375 of "Practical physics" (1922)
Web address: https://farm4.staticflickr.com/3873/14784812262_9374e
3122b_o_d.jpg
Author: Millikan, Robert Andrews Gale, Henry Gordon
Author web address: https://www.flickr.com/photos/
internetarchivebookimages/
Licensed Under: Public Domain

Figure 1.2—Title: Photo of vocalists/actors Joan Weldon and Byron Palmer
Web address: http://commons.wikimedia.org/wiki/File:Joan_Weldon_
Byron_Palmer_1955.jpg
Author: CBS Radio
Licensed Under: Public Domain (1955)

Figure 1.3—Title: Laboratory ultrasonic bath PS 10000
Web address: http://commons.wikimedia.org/wiki/File:Ultrasonic_
bath_1.jpg
Author: Karelj

Author web address: http://commons.wikimedia.org/wiki/User:Karelj
Licensed Under: Public Domain

Figure 1.4—Title: Tsunami
Web address: http://commons.wikimedia.org/wiki/File:The_Great_
Wave_off_Kanagawa.jpg#mediaviewer/File:Tsunami_by_hokusai_19th_
century.jpg
Author: Katsushika Hokusai, 1826
Author web address: Metropolitan Museum of Art
Licensed Under: Public Domain

Figure 1.5—Title: Tuning fork
Web address: https://www.flickr.com/photos/21025851@
N00/2169196138
Author: Eurok
Author web address: https://www.flickr.com/photos/21025851@N00/
Licensed Under: CC by 2.0
License web address: https://creativecommons.org/licenses/by/2.0/

Figure 1.6—Title: vu decibles
Web address: https://farm1.staticflickr.com/156/360249761_7fbfc4db
eb_o_d.jpg
Author: James Keller
Author web address: https://www.flickr.com/photos/semaphoria/
Licensed Under: CC by ND 2.0
License web address: https://creativecommons.org/licenses/by-nd/2.0/

*Figure 1.7—Title: A U.S. Navy McDonnell Douglas F/A-18C Hornet
from Strike Fighter Squadron 195 (VFA-195) Dambusters, Carrier Air*

Wing 5 (CVW-5), Naval Air Station (NAS) Atsugi, Japan (JPN), breaks
the sound barrier during the Freedom through Friendship Air Show at
Osan Air Base (AB), Republic of Korea (KOR).
Web address: http://commons.wikimedia.org/wiki/File:FA18C_breaking_
sound_barrier_2005_-_filtered.jpg
Author: Tsgt. Raheem Moore, USAF
Author web address: http://www.dodmedia.osd.mil/DVIC_View/
Still_Details.cfm?SDAN=DFSD0602979&JPGPath=/Assets/Still/2006/
Air_Force/DF-SD-06-02979.JPG
Licensed Under: Public Domain

Figure 1.8—Title: glassbreak
Web address: https://farm4.staticflickr.com/3598/4081192022_2e79a7
d42f_o_d.jpg
Author: Steven Duong
Author web address: https://www.flickr.com/photos/stevenduong/
Licensed Under: CC by ND 2.0
License web address: https://creativecommons.org/licenses/by-nd/2.0/

Figure 1.9—Title: Image from page 366 of "Autobiography of Charles H.
Spurgeon compiled from his diary, letters and records by his wife and his
private secretary" (1899)
Web address: https://www.flickr.com/photos/
internetarchivebookimages/14776538161/in/photolist-bghMJK-ovKBZk-
bBtiH8-5xp9Hk-owzEYc-owzcpV-8omJwX-4poRma-bGjNPn
Author: Spurgeon, C. H. (Charles Haddon)
Author web address: Passmore and Alabaster Publishers
Licensed Under: Public Domain

Figure 1.10—Title: 50Hz sine wave
Web address: http://commons.wikimedia.org/wiki/File:50Hz_sine.jpg
Author: Sogning
Author web address: http://commons.wikimedia.org/wiki/User:Sogning
Licensed Under: Public Domain

Figure 1.11—Title: 50Hz square wave
Web address: http://commons.wikimedia.org/wiki/File:50Hz_square.jpg
Author: Sogning
Author web address: http://commons.wikimedia.org/wiki/User:Sogning
Licensed Under: Public Domain

Figure 1.12—Title: 50Hz sawtooth wave
Web address: http://commons.wikimedia.org/wiki/File:50Hz_Sawtooth.
jpg
Author: Sogning
Author web address: http://commons.wikimedia.org/wiki/User:Sogning
Licensed Under: Public Domain

Figure 1.13—Title: Radio Diora Aga RSZ50 1
Web address: http://en.wikipedia.org/wiki/Antique_radio#mediaviewer/
File:Radio_Diora_Aga_RSZ50_1.jpg
Author: Wojciech Pysz
Author web address: http://oldradio.pl
Licensed Under: CC by SA 2.5
License web address: http://creativecommons.org/licenses/by-sa/2.5/

Unit 2

Figure 2.1—Title: asuckerforrandom10
Web address: https://farm9.staticflickr.com/8191/8130684544_8797fc
00be_o_d.jpg
Author: Franz Schuier
Author web address: https://www.flickr.com/photos/franzschuier/
Licensed Under: CC by 2.0
License Web Address: https://creativecommons.org/licenses/by/2.0/

Figure 2.2—Title: Louvet Drehleier
Web address: http://en.wikipedia.org/wiki/Hurdy_gurdy#mediaviewer/
File:Louvet_Drehleier.JPG
Author: Frinck51

Author web address: http://commons.wikimedia.org/wiki/User:Frinck51
Licensed Under: CC by SA 3.0
License Web Address: http://creativecommons.org/licenses/by-sa/3.0/

Figure 2.3—Title: Telegraph Key
Web address: http://commons.wikimedia.org/wiki/File:Swiss_Army_
Telegraph_Key.jpeg
Author: Simon A Eugster
Author web address: http://commons.wikimedia.org/wiki/
User:LivingShadow
Licensed Under: CC by SA 3.0
License Web Address: http://creativecommons.org/licenses/by-sa/3.0/

Figure 2.4—Title: Chase & Baker player piano, Buffalo, NY, USA, circa
1885.
Web address: http://commons.wikimedia.org/wiki/File:Chase_%26_
Baker_player_piano,_Buffalo,_NY,_circa_1885.JPG
Author: Daderot
Author web address: http://commons.wikimedia.org/wiki/User:Daderot
Licensed Under: Public Domain

Figure 2.5—Title: Detektivbyran
Web address: http://de.wikipedia.org/wiki/Theremin#mediaviewer/
Datei:Detektivbyr%C3%A5n.jpg
Author: Bengt Nyman
Author web address: http://www.flickr.com/photos/bnsd/3775062641/
Licensed Under: CC by 2.0
License Web Address: http://creativecommons.org/licenses/by/2.0

Figure 2.6—Title: Minimoog (Buffalo Museum of Science)
Web address: http://en.wikipedia.org/wiki/Moog_
synthesizer#mediaviewer/File:Minimoog_%28Buffalo_Museum_of_
Science%29.jpg
Author: Alex Harden
Author web address: http://www.flickr.com/people/24396426@N00
Licensed Under: CC by 2.0
License Web Address: http://creativecommons.org/licenses/by/2.0

Figure 2.7—Title: Fairlight Green Screen
Web address: http://en.wikipedia.org/wiki/Fairlight_CMI#mediaviewer/
File:Fairlight_green_screen.jpg
Author: Starpause kid
Author web address: http://www.flickr.com/photos/k9d/5358777148/
Licensed Under: CC by 2.0
License Web Address: http://creativecommons.org/licenses/by/2.0

Figure 2.8—Title: Computer music piano roll of Beethoven's Ode to Joy.
Web address: http://commons.wikimedia.org/wiki/File:Computer_
music_piano_roll.png
Author: Kanohara
Author web address: http://commons.wikimedia.org/wiki/User:Kanohara
Licensed Under: Public Domain

Figure 2.9—Title: Roland TR-808
Web address: http://commons.wikimedia.org/wiki/File:Roland_TR-
808_%28large%29.jpg
Author: Brandon Daniel
Author web address: http://flickr.com/photos/54581307@N00
Licensed Under: CC by SA 2.0
License Web Address: http://creativecommons.org/licenses/by-sa/2.0/
deed.en

Figure 2.10—Title: Shana (last name unknown) and Jeff McNulty of
BlöödHag in the recording studio at The Vera Project space at Seattle
Center, Seattle, Washington. The Vera Project is an all-ages music and
art center.
Web address: http://commons.wikimedia.org/wiki/File:Vera_
Project_06A.jpg
Author: joe Mabel
Author web address: http://commons.wikimedia.org/wiki/User:Jmabel
Licensed Under: CC by SA 3.0

Figure 2.11—Title: Creating the Tool Song
Web address: http://www.flickr.com/photos/pankaj/146854714/
Author: Pankaj Kaushal
Author web address: http://www.flickr.com/photos/pankaj/
Licensed Under: CC by ND 2.0
License Web Address: https://creativecommons.org/licenses/by-nd/2.0/

Figure 2.12—Title: NI Maschine (closeup)
Web address: http://fr.wikipedia.org/wiki/Native_Instruments_
Maschine#mediaviewer/Fichier:NI_Maschine_%28closeup%29.jpg
Author: Dmitriy G
Author web address: http://www.flickr.com/people/24805317@N07
Licensed Under: CC by SA 2.0
License Web Address: http://creativecommons.org/licenses/by-sa/2.0

Figure 2.13—Title: DJ turntable scratching music hang up disco
Web address: pixabay.com/en/dj-turntable-scratching-music-228999/
Author: phio
Author web address: http://pixabay.com/en/users/phio/
Licensed Under: Public Domain

Unit 3

Figure 3.1—Title: Squier Bullet Special all collors
Web address: http://en.wikipedia.org/wiki/Fender_Bullet#mediaviewer/
File:Squier_Bullet_Special._all_collors.jpg
Author: Aoresteen
Author web address: http://commons.wikimedia.org/w/index.php?title=
User:Aoresteen&action=edit&redlink=1
Licensed Under: CC by SA 3.0
License Web Address: http://creativecommons.org/licenses/by-sa/3.0

Figure 3.2—Title: Title plate of en:The Wonderful Wizard of Oz (not the cover, it's the interior title page), 1900 Wizard
Web address: en.wikipedia.org/wiki/File:Wizard_title_page.jpg
Author: User
Author web address: http://en.wikipedia.org/wiki/User:
Licensed Under: Public Domain

Figure 3.3—Title: Hats, hats, hats...
Web address: http://farm8.staticflickr.com/7025/6522197035_7c5b21
98ba_o_d.jpg
Author: Bob Mical
Author web address: http://www.flickr.com/photos/small_realm/
Licensed Under: CC by 2.0
License Web Address: https://creativecommons.org/licenses/by/2.0/

Figure 3.4—Title: mii
Web address: http://farm1.staticflickr.com/147/365903105_379ad968
16_o_d.png
Author: jimthompson
Author web address: http://www.flickr.com/photos/jimthompson/
Licensed Under: CC by SA 2.0
License Web Address: https://creativecommons.org/licenses/by-sa/2.0/

Figure 3.5—Title: Image from page 209 of "Modern music and musicians: [Encyclopedic]" (1918)
Web address: https://farm6.staticflickr.com/5585/14592840079_25cff0
7241_o_d.jpg
Author: Elson, Louis Charles, 1848-1920
Author web address: New York: The University Society Inc
Licensed Under: Public Domain

Figure 3.6—Title: reel to reel
Web address: https://farm6.staticflickr.com/5096/5427494493_
e49223ed1d_o_d.gif
Author: Generation Bass
Author web address: https://www.flickr.com/photos/generationbass/
Licensed Under: CC by 2.0

License Web Address: https://creativecommons.org/licenses/by/2.0/

Figure 3.7—Title: LP DJ Music Record Player
Web address: http://pixabay.com/en/lp-dj-music-record-player-376549/
Author: niekverlaan
Author web address: http://pixabay.com/en/users/niekverlaan/
Licensed Under: Public Domain

Figure 3.8—Title: Printscreen by Nrgiza—Amen Break Sample Image
Web address: http://commons.wikimedia.org/wiki/File:Amen_break_
sample_image.png
Author: Nrgiza
Author web address: http://en.wikipedia.org/wiki/User:Nrgiza
Licensed Under: Public Domain

Unit 4

Figure 4.1—Title: Gramophone 1914
Web address: http://commons.wikimedia.org/wiki/
File:Gramophone_1914.png
Author: Publisher Eino Louhivuori, the author of the image itself anonymous
Licensed Under: Public Domain

Figure 4.2—Title: Portrait of French typographer Édouard-Léon Scott de Martinville (1817-1879), inventor of the phonautograph.
Web address: http://commons.wikimedia.org/wiki/File%3AEdouard-
L%C3%A9on_Scott_de_Martinville.jpg
Author: Unknown
Licensed Under: Public Domain

Figure 4.3—Title: Image from page 857 of "The new international encyclopaedia" (1905)
Web address: https://farm3.staticflickr.com/2917/14781572442_24a77
ffcb5_o_d.jpg
Author: Gilman, Daniel Coit, 1831-1908 Peck, Harry Thurston, 1856-
1914 Colby, Frank Moore, 1865-1925
Author web address: New York: Dodd, Mead
Licensed Under: Public Domain

Figure 4.4—Title: Edison Gold Moulded Cylinder Record, ca. 1904
Web address: http://commons.wikimedia.org/wiki/
File:Edisongoldmoulded.jpg
Author: Phonatic
Author web address: http://en.wikipedia.org/wiki/User:Phonatic
Licensed Under: GNU Free Doc License
License Web Address: http://commons.wikimedia.org/wiki/GNU_Free_
Documentation_License

Figure 4.5—Title: needle
Web address: https://farm1.staticflickr.
com/27/39962952_262bb9ebf3_o_d.jpg
Author: Peyri Herrera
Author web address: https://www.flickr.com/photos/peyri/
Licensed Under: CC by ND 2.0
License Web Address: https://creativecommons.org/licenses/by-nd/2.0/

Figure 4.6—Title: Disco de pasta de 10 pulgadas y 78 RPM
Web address: http://commons.wikimedia.org/wiki/File:Disco_de_78_
RPM.jpg
Author: Banfield
Author web address: http://commons.wikimedia.org/wiki/User:Banfield
Licensed Under: Public Domain

Figure 4.7—Title: Antique Box Collectible Electronic Historical
Web address: pixabay.com/en/antique-box-collectible-electronic-21893/
Author: PublicDomainPictures
Author web address: http://pixabay.com/en/users/
PublicDomainPictures/
Licensed Under: Public Domain

Figure 4.8—Title: IMG_1321
Web address: https://farm4.staticflickr.com/3342/3502619520_362c24
0d4f_o_d.jpg
Author: s_p_a_c_e_m_a_n
Author web address: https://www.flickr.com/photos/s_p_a_c_e_m_a_n/
Licensed Under: CC by 2.0
License Web Address: https://creativecommons.org/licenses/by/2.0/

Figure 4.9—Title: relics of a bgone age—8-Track
Web address: https://farm4.staticflickr.com/3789/11645555664_8e7a7
79fd9_o_d.jpg
Author: Paul Townsend
Author web address: https://www.flickr.com/photos/
brizzlebornandbred/
Licensed Under: CC by ND 2.0
License Web Address: https://creativecommons.org/licenses/by-nd/2.0/

Figure 4.10—Title: Cassette Sony
Web address: https://farm1.staticflickr.com/84/269393517_
b826beea65_o_d.jpg
Author: Esparta Palma
Author web address: https://www.flickr.com/photos/esparta/
Licensed Under: CC by ND 2.0
License Web Address: https://creativecommons.org/licenses/by-nd/2.0/

Figure 4.11—Title: Compact Disc
Web address: http://ro.wikipedia.org/wiki/Disc_compact#mediaviewer/
Fi%C8%99ier:Compact_Disc.jpg
Author: Arun Kulshreshtha
Author web address: Unknown
Licensed Under: CC by SA 2.5
License Web Address: http://creativecommons.org/licenses/by-sa/2.5

Figure 4.12—Title: Photo of the iPod video, iPod nano 2 GB andiPod
shuffle 2 GB.
Web address: http://commons.wikimedia.org/wiki/File:IPod_5G,_
nano_2G,_shuffle_2G.jpg
Author: User: HereToHelp
Author web address: http://commons.wikimedia.org/wiki/
User:HereToHelp
Licensed Under: Public Domain

Unit 5

Figure 5.1—Title: Midi Ports and Cable
Web address: http://en.wikipedia.org/wiki/MIDI#mediaviewer/File:Midi_
ports_and_cable.jpg
Author::en:Pretzelpaws
Author web address: http://en.wikipedia.org/wiki/User:Pretzelpaws
Licensed Under: CC by SA 3.0
License Web Address: http://creativecommons.org/licenses/by-sa/3.0/

Figure 5.2—Title: Roland TD-20
Web address: https://farm4.staticflickr.com/3049/2940141998_
d6189d8311_o_d.jpg
Author: Derek Purdy
Author web address: https://www.flickr.com/photos/dpurdy/
Licensed Under: CC by ND 2.0
License Web Address: https://creativecommons.org/licenses/by-nd/2.0/

Figure 5.3—Title: A 5 pin DIN connector of a PC keyboard
Web address: http://commons.wikimedia.org/wiki/File:DIN_Keyboard_
Connector.jpg
Author: Michael Krahe
Author web address: http://de.wikipedia.org/wiki/Benutzer:MichiK
Licensed Under: CC by SA 3.0
License Web Address: http://creativecommons.org/licenses/by-sa/3.0/
deed.en

Figure 5.4—Title: Midi Interface—Web address: https://farm4.

staticflickr.com/3751/12778513493_6ffb83428b_o_d.jpg
Author: David J
Author web address: https://www.flickr.com/photos/sebilden/
Licensed Under: CC by 2.0
License Web Address: https://creativecommons.org/licenses/by/2.0/

Figure 5.5—Title: Sibelius 6
Web address: http://es.wikipedia.org/wiki/Sibelius_%28programa%29#
mediaviewer/Archivo:Sibelius_6.png
Author: Areapianoemc
Author web address: http://commons.wikimedia.org/w/index.php?title=
User:Areapianoemc&action=edit&redlink=1
Licensed Under: CC by 3.0
License Web Address: http://creativecommons.org/licenses/by/3.0

Figure 5.6—Title: Onyx the Digital Pied Piper
Web address: http://en.wikipedia.org/wiki/Wind_
controller#mediaviewer/File:Onyx_The_Digital_Pied_Piper.jpg
Author: Vlad Spears
Author web address: http://www.flickr.com/people/83939749@N00
Licensed Under: CC by SA 2.0
License Web Address: http://creativecommons.org/licenses/by-sa/2.0

Figure 5.7
Title: Et Marquee 2
Web address: http://en.wikipedia.org/wiki/Stage_lighting#mediaviewer/
File:Et_marquee_2.JPG
Author: Lekogm
Author web address: http://en.wikipedia.org/wiki/User:Lekogm
Licensed Under: CC by SA 2.5
License Web Address: http://creativecommons.org/licenses/by-sa/2.5

Figure 5.8—Title: Guitar Hero series controllers
Web address: http://en.wikipedia.org/wiki/Rhythm_game_
accessories#mediaviewer/File:Guitar_Hero_series_controllers.jpg
Author: Y2kcrazyjoker4
Author web address: http://en.wikipedia.org/wiki/User:Y2kcrazyjoker4
Licensed Under: Public Domain

Unit 6

Figure 6.1—Title: Play art abstract guitar music rock rock-n-roll
Web address: http://pixabay.com/en/play-art-abstract-guitar-
music-69992/
Author: PublicDomainPictures
Author web address: http://pixabay.com/en/users/
PublicDomainPictures/
Licensed Under: Public Domain

Figure 6.2—Title: Accord Acoustic Art Background Classical Culture
Web address: http://pixabay.com/en/accord-acoustic-art-
background-2119/
Author: PublicDomainPictures
Author web address: http://pixabay.com/en/users/
PublicDomainPictures/
Licensed Under: Public Domain

Figure 6.3—Title: New Winding 1
Web address: http://farm4.staticflickr.com/3589/3511734651_2d4c82
006f_o_d.jpg
Author: 1Roadside Guitars
Author web address: http://www.flickr.com/photos/roadsideguitars/
Licensed Under: CC by SA 2.0
License Web Address: https://creativecommons.org/licenses/by-sa/2.0/

Figure 6.4—Title: Elektrofryingpan
Web address: http://en.wikipedia.org/wiki/Frying_
pan_%28guitar%29#mediaviewer/File:Elektrofryingpan.jpg
Author: Museum of Making Music
Author web address: http://en.wikipedia.org/wiki/User:Museum_of_

Making_Music
Licensed Under: CC by 3.0
License Web Address: http://creativecommons.org/licenses/by/3.0

Figure 6.5—Title: Pedalboard (995939579)
Web address: http://commons.wikimedia.org/wiki/
File:Pedalboard_%28995939579%29.jpg
Author: Michael Morel
Author web address: http://www.flickr.com/people/21026676@N00
Licensed Under: CC by 2.0
License Web Address: http://creativecommons.org/licenses/by/2.0/
deed.en

Figure 6.6—Title: Les Paul, ca Jan 1947 (William P Gottlieb 07001)
Web address: http://en.wikipedia.org/wiki/Les_Paul#mediaviewer/
File:Les_Paul,_ca._Jan._1947_%28William_P._Gottlieb_07001%29.jpg
Author: William P Gottlieb
Author web address: http://en.wikipedia.org/wiki/William_P._Gottlieb
Licensed Under: Public Domain

Figure 6.7—Title: Chuck Berry 1971
Web address: http://en.wikipedia.org/wiki/Chuck_Berry#mediaviewer/
File:Chuck_Berry_1971.JPG
Author: Universal Attractions (management) Publicity photo
Licensed Under: Public Domain

Figure 6.8—Title: Velvet Elvis Presley painting
Web address: http://en.wikipedia.org/wiki/Velvet_Elvis#mediaviewer/
File:Velvet_Elvis_Presley_painting.jpg
Author: Jamie Dwyer
Author web address: http://www.flickr.com/photos/
jamidwyer/2474408252/
Licensed Under: CC by SA 2.0
License Web Address: http://creativecommons.org/licenses/by-sa/2.0

Figure 6.9—Title: Jimi Hendrix 1967 uncropped
Web address: http://en.wikipedia.org/wiki/Jimi_hendrix#mediaviewer/
File:Jimi_Hendrix_1967_uncropped.jpg
Author: Original photographer unknown - e24.se, attributed to Scanpix
trelleborgsallehanda.se
Licensed Under: Public Domain

Figure 6.10—Title: Heavy Metal Fire
Web address: http://aerokay.deviantart.com/art/Heavy-Metal-Fire-
268695531#comments
Author: aerokay
Author web address: http://aerokay.deviantart.com/
Licensed Under: CC by 3.0
License Web Address: http://creativecommons.org/licenses/by/3.0/

Figure 6.11—Title: Wave Gotik Treffen 2007
Web address: http://en.wikipedia.org/wiki/Punk_fashion#mediaviewer/
File:Wave_Gotik_Treffen_2007.jpg
Author: Grant Mitchell
Author web address: http://www.flickr.com/people/48683366@N00
Licensed Under: CC by 2.0
License Web Address: http://creativecommons.org/licenses/by/2.0

Figure 6.12—Title: Dr Martens, black, old
Web address: http://en.wikipedia.org/wiki/Dr._Martens#mediaviewer/
File:Dr_Martens,_black,_old.jpg
Author: Aavindraa
Author web address: http://commons.wikimedia.org/wiki/
User:Aavindraa
Licensed Under: CC by SA 3.0
License Web Address: http://creativecommons.org/licenses/by-sa/3.0/

Figure 6.13—Title: The Bass Man
Web address: http://farm3.staticflickr.com/2937/14565956170_97c4fb
4c32_o_d.jpg
Author: swong95765

Author web address: http://www.flickr.com/photos/29487672@N07/
Licensed Under: CC by 2.0
License Web Address: https://creativecommons.org/licenses/by/2.0/

Figure 6.14—Title: Korg RK-100
Web address: http://en.wikipedia.org/wiki/Keytar#mediaviewer/
File:Korg_RK-100.jpg
Author: Clusternote
Author web address: http://commons.wikimedia.org/wiki/
User:Clusternote
Licensed Under: CC by 2.0
License Web Address: http://creativecommons.org/licenses/by/2.0

Figure 6.15—Title: A Gibson Les Paul Classic Premium Plus electric
guitar in Trans Amber.
Web address: http://commons.wikimedia.org/wiki/File:Gibson_LP_
Classic.png
Author: Patrick Despoix
Author web address: http://commons.wikimedia.org/wiki/User:Piso17
Licensed Under: CC by SA 2.5
License Web Address: http://creativecommons.org/licenses/by-sa/2.5/
deed.en

Unit 7

Figure 7.1—Title: Speakers Sound Audio Speaker Entertainment Concert
Web address: http://pixabay.com/en/speakers-sound-audio-
speaker-309753/
Author: Nemo
Author web address: http://pixabay.com/en/speakers-sound-audio-
speaker-309753/
Licensed Under: Public Domain

Figure 7.2—Title: Shure SM58
Web address: http://en.wikipedia.org/wiki/Shure_SM58#mediaviewer/
File:Shure_SM58.jpg
Author: Iain Fergussun
Author web address: http://commons.wikimedia.org/wiki/User:Iainf
Licensed Under: CC by 2.5
License Web Address: http://creativecommons.org/licenses/by/2.5

Figure 7.3—Title: Janet Jackson
Web address: http://en.wikipedia.org/wiki/Rhythm_Nation_%28influenc
e%29#mediaviewer/File:Janet_jackson.png
Author: Bahamutskingdom
Author web address: http://commons.wikimedia.org/w/index.php?title=
User:Bahamutskingdom&action=edit&redlink=1
Licensed Under: CC by SA 3.0
License Web Address: http://creativecommons.org/licenses/by-sa/3.0

Figure 7.4—Title: Audio Technica AT831R photo 1
Web address: https://farm5.staticflickr.com/4076/4786598398_55c268
7958_o_d.jpg
Author: Audio-Technica
Author web address: https://www.flickr.com/photos/audio-technica/
Licensed Under: CC by ND 2.0
License Web Address: https://creativecommons.org/licenses/by-nd/2.0/

Figure 7.5—Title: EPP Summit October 2010
Web address: http://commons.wikimedia.org/wiki/File:Flickr_-_
europeanpeoplesparty_-_EPP_Summit_October_2010_%285%29.jpg
Author: European People's Party
Author web address: http://www.flickr.com/photos/45198836@N04
Licensed Under: CC by 2.0
License Web Address: http://creativecommons.org/licenses/by/2.0/
deed.en

Figure 7.6.1—Title: New Sennheiser G3 W100 Wireless System
including a Rode Reporter microphone
Web address: http://commons.wikimedia.org/wiki/File:Sennheiser_

Unit 8

Author web address: http://commons.wikimedia.org/wiki/
User:Gobonobo
Licensed Under: CC by 2.0
License Web Address: http://creativecommons.org/licenses/by/2.0

Figure 8.8—Title: Afrika Bambaataa and DJ Yutaka (2004)
Web address: http://en.wikipedia.org/wiki/File:AFRIKA.jpg
Author: Sean Wilson/Sean-Jin
Author web address: http://en.wikipedia.org/wiki/User:Sean-Jin
Licensed Under: Public Domain

Figure 8.9—Title: Run DMC Adidas
Web address: http://commons.wikimedia.org/wiki/File:Run_DMC_
Adidas.jpg
Author: User: rrafson/Bata Shoe Museum Toronto ON
Author web address: http://commons.wikimedia.org/w/index.php?title=
User:Rrafson&action=edit&redlink=1
Licensed Under: CC by SA 3.0
License Web Address: http://creativecommons.org/licenses/by-sa/3.0/
deed.en

Figure 8.10—Title: Flavor-flav
Web address: http://commons.wikimedia.org/wiki/File:Flavor-flav.jpg
Author: Darian Cabot
Author web address: http://commons.wikimedia.org/w/index.php?title=
User:MrQuan&action=edit&redlink=1
Licensed Under: Public Domain

Figure 8.11—Title: Akai MPC60
Web address: http://en.wikipedia.org/wiki/Akai#mediaviewer/File:Akai_
MPC60.jpg
Author: Kimi95
Author web address: http://it.wikipedia.org/wiki/User:Kimi95
Licensed Under: CC by 3.0
License Web Address: http://creativecommons.org/licenses/by/3.0

Figure 8.12—Title: Autotuneevo6
Web address: http://en.wikipedia.org/wiki/Auto_tune#mediaviewer/
File:Autotuneevo6.jpg
Author: Dashbot screenshot from GarageBand
Author web address: http://en.wikipedia.org/wiki/User:DASHBot
Licensed Under: Fair Use

Unit 9

Figure 9.1—What if Aliens Listen to CDs and Not Records?
Web address: https://farm3.staticflickr.com/2504/3698187983_
ab48e2b7c3_o_d.jpg
Author: Chuck Coker
Author web address : https://www.flickr.com/photos/caveman_92223/
Licensed Under: CC by ND 2.0
License Web Address: https://creativecommons.org/licenses/by-nd/2.0/

Figure 9.2—Roll of Cash
Web address: http://www.flickr.com/photos/68751915@
N05/6355261479
Author: 401(K) 2012
Author web address : http://www.flickr.com/photos/68751915@N05/
Licensed Under: CC by SA 2.0
License Web Address: https://creativecommons.org/licenses/by-sa/2.0/

Figure 9.3—Pic 1 Police Transfer
Web address: https://farm7.staticflickr.com/6234/6290299189_58d5c7
1c30_o_d.jpg
Author: NATO Training Mission –AF…
Author web address : https://www.flickr.com/photos/ntm-a_cstc-a/
Licensed Under: CC by SA 2.0
License Web Address: https://creativecommons.org/licenses/by-sa/2.0/

Figure 9.4—Businessman Man Silhouette Business Businessmen
Web address: http://pixabay.com/en/businessman-man-silhouette-
business-296833/
Author: Nemo
Author web address : http://pixabay.com/en/users/Nemo/
Licensed Under: Public Domain

Figure 9.5—Music Studio Mixer
Web address: http://splitshire.com/music-studio-mixer/
Author: Splitshire
Author web address : http://splitshire.com/author/splitshare/
Licensed Under: Public Domain

Figure 9.6—Money Wings Eco
Web address: http://pixabay.com/en/money-wings-eco-48103/
Author: Nemo
Author web address : http://pixabay.com/en/users/Nemo/
Licensed Under: Public Domain

Figure 9.7—Coach Bus Red Transport Travel Transportation
Web address: http://pixabay.com/en/coach-bus-red-transport-
travel-303659/
Author: Nemo
Author web address : http://pixabay.com/en/users/Nemo/
Licensed Under: Public Domain

Figure 9.8—Mouse Globe clean Internet World Wide Web www
Web address: http://pixabay.com/en/mouse-globe-clean-
internet-306274/
Author: Nemo
Author web address : http://pixabay.com/en/users/Nemo/
Licensed Under: Public Domain

Figure 9.9—Party Dancing Dancer Disco Seventies Music
Web address: http://pixabay.com/en/party-dancing-dancer-
disco-146582/
Author: OpenClips
Author web address : http://pixabay.com/en/users/OpenClips/
Licensed Under: Public Domain

Figure 9.10—Woman Face Head Question Mark Circle Tree
Web address: http://pixabay.com/en/woman-face-head-question-
mark-241327/
Author: geralt
Author web address : http://pixabay.com/en/users/geralt/
Licensed Under: Public Domain

Unit 10

Figure 10.1—DJ Gramophone Party Shout Music
Web address: http://pixabay.com/en/dj-gramophone-party-shout-
music-101783/
Author: fotobias
Author web address : http://pixabay.com/en/users/fotobias/
Licensed Under: Public Domain

Figure 10.2—Behringer dx626 1
Web address: http://commons.wikimedia.org/wiki/File:Behringer_
dx626_1.jpg
Author: PJ
Author web address : http://commons.wikimedia.org/wiki/User:PJ
Licensed Under: CC by SA 3.0
License Web Address: http://creativecommons.org/licenses/by-sa/3.0/
deed.en

Figure 10.3—Technics SL-1200MK2-2
Web address: http://en.wikipedia.org/wiki/Technics_SL-
1200#mediaviewer/File:Technics_SL-1200MK2-2.jpg
Author: 32bitmaschine
Author web address : http://commons.wikimedia.org/wiki/
User:32bitmaschine
Licensed Under: CC by SA 2.5
License Web Address: http://creativecommons.org/licenses/by-sa/2.5